COLLEGIAL
COACHING

Research for the Practitioner

Other Titles in This Series:

COLLEGIAL COACHING:

INTO THE TEACHING SELF

SECOND EDITION

Marylou Dantonio

Phi Delta Kappa
Bloomington, Indiana

Phi Delta Kappa International, Bloomington, Indiana 47402-0789
Phi Delta Kappa Inc.
© 1995, 2001 by Phi Delta Kappa
All rights reserved. First edition 1995
Second edition 2001
Printed in the United States of America

Library of Congress Catalog Card Number: 2001093503
ISBN 0-87367-732-3

To my mother, Louise Marie DiNucci, and
my father, Eugene Raymond Dantonio,
whose gifts to me were courage and love.

CONTENTS

Part Two: Practice

Part Three: Collegial Inquiry

PREFACE TO THE SECOND EDITION

My work over the past 30 years has brought me face to face with teachers struggling with professional development. In talking with teachers across the country, I sense that they possess a growing desire to free themselves from the prevailing, traditional school culture that can isolate them and bind their growth and development. A school culture that does not recognize that teachers, like students, are in a process of continual growth and development impedes both the development of teaching excellence and student achievement.

Teachers need time to practice their art and craft together. They need diverse opportunities to practice important instructional methods together so that they can effect the best learning opportunities for students in their classrooms. Practice opportunities require time for teachers to reflect upon and analyze instructional techniques and strategies. Teachers need to be supported in their attempts to grow and to develop excellence in their delivery of instruction. Excellence in instructional delivery is the result of hours of rehearsal in which teachers investigate methods that are appropriate for the children they teach. In short, teachers must prepare and study their instruction utilizing self-study methods and engaging in collegial dialogue prior to their classroom delivery. Studying and interacting about effective instructional methods can revitalize learning for students and renew teachers' sense of professionalism.

However, embedded within many school cultures are constricting elements that thwart the emergence of nurturing, developmental structures. First, evaluation of teachers is too often perceived as the sole means for improving teaching. The fear of receiving a poor evaluation can inhibit teachers so they feel little freedom to "try on" unfamiliar instructional practices. Second, the demanding schedule of teaching class after class of students leaves little room for reflection on oneself as a teacher and the instructional processes one uses to educate. Third, the lack of safe environments in which teachers can rehearse different instructional practices to acquire expertise before using them results in teachers doing what is most familiar and comfortable. And, most importantly, the dearth of opportunities for sharing ideas and collaborating in the school setting restrains teachers from reaching out to each other for help. If educators are going to provide optimum learning opportunities for students, then attention must be given to ways in which teachers evolve in the practice of teaching.

Teachers who view their roles as confined by the boundaries of their students in their classrooms, who do not take the liberty to explore the contributions they can make to the teaching profession by working with other teachers for the greater good of students, and who do not perceive themselves as capable instructional leaders in their own right defeat the emergence of self-directed development that nourishes their further growth as professionals. The issue of how to develop and refine oneself as a teacher in a school culture that restricts professional growth and development through the regimentation of staff development and the confines of evaluation requires that teachers step out of these confines to study and to experiment with new instructional practices. Courageously, they must find ways to engage in rehearsal sessions and collegial inquiry. In the process, schools can evolve into a culture of learning for all who participate. Toward this end, two new chapters, Professional Inquiry and Collegial Self-Study and Collegial Action Self-Study Groups, have been added to this second edition.

Anne Lieberman and Lynne Miller note that "teaching remains messy, complex, and recursive work. It is still more of art that science. Nevertheless, the transitions that teachers are making hold great promise for rethinking and clarifying what it means to be a teacher."[1] The transitions from teaching in isolation to building professional communities, from teaching as a form of technical work to teaching as a form of inquiry into practice, and from teaching as work that is controlled by others to teacher leadership that informs schooling practices require educators to create learning opportunities to study teaching practice. The study of how we develop as classroom teachers necessitates not only that we inquire into our own instructional practices, but also that we assist our fellow classroom educators in expanding their repertoire of instructional methods. As a result, we build common understandings about teaching and learning that impact the school's curriculum, as well as enrich our own practice.

It has been my experience that teachers thrive when they succeed in emancipating themselves from the traditional enculturation of their teaching roles. The collegial coaching process can be used to create opportunities for developing personal insights about learning, to encourage trust among classroom educators so they can share knowledge about instruction, and to engage in self-study and collaborative research to refine instructional practices. The process presented in this book provides a means for teachers to study both themselves as teachers and the instructional process. It is based on my own continual inquiry and growth as a teacher. It continues to evolve as I share it with other teachers in schools, both as a colleague and a teacher educator. The scope of the collegial coaching process has grown from one-on-one partnership learning to self-study groups. Collegial coaching is best suited to teachers who desire to take charge of their own professional development and who aspire to influence talent development among their colleagues. Such teachers are the innovators of education.

Who are these innovator teachers? They are teachers and teacher educators whose instinctive artistry in teaching is the fertile ground for assisting other teachers in actively pursuing their own professional development. They are everyday teachers and teachers of teachers whose commitment transcends their classrooms and their schools. They are guided by an innate sense of timing and do not easily fit into the status quo of schools. They survive in spite of forces to conform to embedded traditions of practicality and isolation. Working together as colleagues, they flourish by building on their teaching strengths and instructional ideas.

Such teachers lead wherever they find themselves, bringing forth vivid, contemporary designs for the study of instructional practices. They continue to develop no matter how frequently or feverishly they are challenged. At times—most of the time—they are nuisances to administrators trained to maintain the status quo.

Innovator teachers recognize that it is difficult to assist other teachers in their development and provide leadership to a profession that has been struck blow after blow by well-intentioned critics. They are sensitive to the effects of years of teacher bashing, recognizing that teachers have been demeaned so that they have little vision as to the powerful impact they can have on the school system and the development of their profession. They understand that it is teachers who must break loose and challenge traditions that confine rather than free spirits for self-growth and empowered leadership.

When innovative teachers collaborate, they create a framework for teacher development that is devoid of hierarchy. Such a framework is collegial; it spirals upward as teachers strive toward completion. It reminds us of Eudora Welty's words:

> It is our inward journey that leads us through time—forward or back, seldom in a straight line, most often spiraling. Each of us is moving, changing, with respect to others. As we discover, we remember, remembering, we discover; and most intensely do we experience this when our separate journeys converge. Our living experience at those meeting points is one of the charged dramatic fields. . . .[2]

In their collegial network, relationships with other teachers are valued. No boundaries bar their development and their work with others. They take a professional journey guided and nurtured by stories, events, opportunities, victories, pivotal points, and self-renewal. Their development is a fluid, relational process acknowledging each teacher's inner wisdom about needs and aspirations for growth. As teachers celebrate their self-determination to grow, they awaken the consciousness of other teachers whose spirits have been broken. More teachers aspire to become a part of the community and network of colleagues engaged in professional practice and development.

Innovative teachers strive to create rich learning environments for teacher growth and do not relinquish their principles, principles derived from one basic purpose: To talk, to share, to inspire, to work with other teachers in order to more fully realize their teaching selves and the impact excellence in instruction has upon the students they serve. Through this process, a network among teachers is formed—from the bottom up, through the root system. Teaching practices evolve; the seeds of collegiality are carried and cultivated by other teachers. The process occurs one teacher at a time, each trusting enough to share her or his teaching self with another teacher.

What are the collegial seeds? One is collaboration. By collaborating, teachers break the isolation so feverishly embedded in schools. Collaboration insures cultivation of the creative inspiration needed to keep growing.

Second is self-direction. Teachers must take charge of and engender their own personal and professional journey of growth. Self-direction means that teachers know deep inside that they have the ability to become artist teachers and that they possess the leadership talent to assist other teachers in their self-development.

Trust is the third collegial seed—trusting oneself to guide one's personal and professional growth, trusting that there are other teachers, like oneself, who are willing to collaborate about teaching and to share strengths and areas for development. Teachers who establish warm, trusting relationships with other teachers are the founders of emerging collegial networks.

Inquiry—collecting information about instructional practice is the fourth seed. Reflecting upon and analyzing both the delivery and effects of instruction contribute to developing sound theory through practice. Teachers who continually refine instruction through self-study and collegial dialogue have greater opportunities for establishing school cultures that succeed in enhancing learning opportunities for everyone.

Commitment is next. It is knowing that wherever teachers find themselves, under diverse circumstances with all kinds of experiences, they can and will be successful as teachers. Teachers must believe in themselves to inspire others. As teachers lead in assisting others on journeys of development, they acknowledge that development is an internal process, originating within.

Developing one's teaching self is a gradual process. Learning about teaching requires teachers to be students of teaching *and* learning. It means practicing the craft of teaching by taking one step at a time, by engaging the assistance of others who possess teaching qualities one wants to refine or emulate. It means knowing when to lead and when to follow. By sharing ideas, problems, and solutions, teachers build morale, reduce feelings of isolation, and empower each other to grow and to lead in most appealing ways. Inquiring into one's self as a teacher and investigating how other teachers' practices can effect a successful repertoire of focused, coherent instructional practices for all renews the school learning culture. Thus, teachers garner effective, self-informed classroom practices for children—the center of our professional lives.

Many people have been active forces in the development of the collegial coaching process and the writing of this book. The love, support, and nurturance of countless individuals have resulted in my determination to engage in this process. I wish to acknowledge the teacher mentors of the Urban Partnerships for Teacher Development Professional Development Sites who believe so strongly in the collegial coaching process that they use it willingly and consistently. It is through their sharing of the process, their insights about the subtlety of its application to specific school settings, and their commitment to the development of teachers that I am able to appreciate the power of the collegial coaching process.

I am especially grateful to have shared teaching and coaching experiences with Katie

Rovaris and Melba Venison, Orleans, Louisiana, public school teachers and University of New Orleans clinical liaison mentors. Without a doubt they are most perceptive educators. I value their expertise as teachers and insights as collegial coaches.

I am deeply indebted to my doctoral students, Patricia Speeg, Aurora King, Glenda Hembree, Cindy Ybos, Betty Lazarus, Holly Broom, and Amanda Martin, among others. I greatly appreciate the research projects documenting the effects of collegial coaching in schools and other institutional settings.

More recently, I have been studying teaching and learning by initiating professional learning communities. My work at Southwest State University in Minnesota has enriched my understanding of the collegial coaching process. This opportunity has re-framed the collegial coaching process as a vital strategy for collaborative teacher research and self-study.

Two other individuals are especially important to me in the development of the collegial coaching process. Edgar Cobett was my first coach in education. From him, I learned that teaching is important life work. It was his belief in me that spearheaded my interest in teacher development. Likewise, I wish to thank Duane Richards for providing opportunities for me to develop and refine the collegial coaching process. His confidence in me in the early years of my career as an educator helped me believe in my teaching self.

I wish to thank my editor, Carol Langdon, for her willingness to take on this project, for her enthusiasm and patience as I shared ideas with her, and for her editing expertise. Carol has become a valued and trusted colleague. She is one of those rare editors who can see into an author's ideas, cut away the garbage, and leave the emerging beauty. My experiences working with her and Phi Delta Kappa have been gratifying and productive. Likewise, I thank Phil Harris for promoting my work in collegial coaching.

Finally, I wish to acknowledge the sacrifices made by my family. My husband, Paul Beisenherz, delayed his writing in order to parent our son while I wrote. My son, Christopher, spent many hours trying to understand my preoccupation with a computer rather than with him. I know that I am blessed to have their love and support. To both of them, I promise my love and attention.

Notes

1. Anne Lieberman and Lynne Miller, *Teachers Transforming Their World and Their Work* (New York: Teachers College Press, 1999), p. 23.

2. Eudora Welty, *One Writer's Beginnings* (Cambridge, Mass.: Warner Books, Inc., 1984), p. 112.

Part One
Theory

CHAPTER ONE

Introduction

When professionals "practice," they do so in a safe context where they can make mistakes, study themselves, and share learning with each other to create excellence in their delivery. Why, then, as professional educators do we use our students in our classrooms as guinea pigs for our "practice"? Why do we fail to provide sustained time to reflect upon, study, and build our instructional repertoire? Why do we confine professional dialogue to defending unexamined assumptions about teaching and learning?

Encouraging professional development and rewarding leadership among teachers are two of the most challenging aspects of education today. In this book, I invite the reader to think differently and creatively about the professional growth of classroom practitioners. I ask you to examine assumptions about teaching and learning. I bring to light professional development as reflective and communal. I promote collegial ways of enhancing instruction, refining teacher leadership skills, and engaging in collaborative research through practice and dialogue.

Collegial coaching is premised on the belief that the growth and development of teaching expertise depends on connectedness, trust and shared visions, common values and goals, and respectful inquiry into theory and practice among individuals within a profession. Inherent in the use of such a professional development model is the assumption that all educators within a school community are knowledgeable and capable, that they are committed to the idea of making a contribution to the development of other professional educators, and that inquiry into themselves as professionals and their practices is crucial to creating excellence in learning. Thus, collegial coaching differs from staff development and inservice education, implemented hierarchically in most schools, by encouraging leadership from and among teachers. It is a person-to-person, collegial, horizontal model. And while it can be a system-wide initiative, collegial coaching is usually brought about teacher by teacher and school by school.

The development and refinement of teaching talent and expertise cultivated through collegial coaching is similar to the talent development process used by performing artists. It encourages teachers to share ideas, concentrate on techniques, and experiment instructionally without being judged by supervisors. As teachers coach each other, they address teaching strengths and weaknesses. It is the teacher desiring to be coached, not a supervisor or principal, who identifies the focus of talents to be developed. As teachers implement collegial coaching, they also work toward creating trusting, nurturing, communal support networks. Collegial coaching is a collaborative, self-initiating, egalitarian way for teachers to develop professionally. Judgments about instructional effectiveness and decisions about how to change come from the teacher.

Six premises contribute to the success of a collegial coaching program:

• No one can force another person to change his or her teaching behavior.
• Improving teaching behavior relies on objective and descriptive reporting of the behavior.
• Reflective practices and problem solving are ongoing processes of professional growth.
• Collaboration among educators in a school community is a process of attraction.
• Time for teacher collaboration is important enough to be included in the school schedule.
• Collegial inquiry is necessary for bringing about renewal in teaching and learning.

For administrators, instituting an effective collegial coaching program often requires enterprise in managing school time and space. Attention must be given to teachers' working conditions, such as finding time in the school day for teachers to coach and locating space for conferences. Likewise, administrators must be open-minded about teachers studying together, making and correcting mistakes in practice, and engaging in collegial and individual study of instructional methods that are appropriate for the school context. More importantly, administrators must be advocates for the collegial coaching process by empowering teachers to determine and to shape their own professional growth plans. This requires that they first trust the talents and commitment of teachers. Their role is to encourage initiatives by individual teachers and groups of teachers to study teaching collaboratively.

The professional development process explored in this book begins inside the teacher. It is a reflective, problem-solving process. Collegial coaching is *teacher* driven. Unlike traditional staff development, where others specify the conditions and expectations necessary for growth, teachers determine what talents must be developed and how these will be developed and practiced. Teachers take responsibility for improving their instructional delivery. They do this through various types of rehearsals that refine their instructional talents. Staff development, on the other hand, is a function of a school system's overall plan for instructional improvement, of which collegial coaching may be a part.

This process challenges teacher isolation—so prevalent in schools—by replacing it with collaborative structures designed by both teachers and administrators. Collegial coaching encourages teachers to be the driving force in school renewal. Establishing collegial relationships among teachers facilitates meaningful and continuing opportunities for school communities to experiment with and inquire into the study of teaching and learning and to rehearse instruction prior to implementing it in classroom situations.

The ideas presented in this book have evolved from my work with teachers in a variety of schools. I am deeply grateful to them for their openness in experimenting with collegial coaching. I remain inspired by their commitment to improve their instructional talents while establishing collegial partnerships.

To many, especially educators schooled in top-down bureaucratic structures, this process will appear foreign, alien, even anarchistic. But, while challenging some ingrained assumptions about how teachers develop their professional talents, this approach can provide administrators with an alternative for assisting teachers in professional growth. This is not to say that collegial coaching is the only way for teachers to develop their talents and leadership skills; however, it has been my experience that collegial coaching offers teachers a way of looking at their professional development that is both exciting and rewarding.

Organization of the Book

It is my intent to describe a process that acts as a catalyst and inspires educators to explore and become involved in other options for collaborative development. In order to assist schools in implementing this form of professional development, this second edition is divided into three sections. The first, Theory, surveys the literature on various aspects and issues related to collegial coaching as a model for developing teaching talent. Bruce Locklear, an insightful colleague, has revised chapters seven, Supervision and Evaluation, and eight, Administrator's Role. His background as a principal and superintendent adds another perspective on how collegial coaching can be used to cultivate and nourish a culture of growth through school practitioner learning. The second part, Practice, provides specific techniques for implementing collegial coaching. The third, new section, Collegial Inquiry, enlarges the scope of the collegial coaching process as a means for engaging in collective teacher research. Using collegial inquiry to study instructional contexts and to refine instruction protects school-based practitioners' right to contribute to building informed theory through practice. Most importantly, it transforms our thinking about how individuals grow as educators.

CHAPTER TWO

Teacher Professional Development

What is missing from the knowledge base for teaching . . . are the voices of teachers themselves, the questions teachers ask, the way teachers use writing and intentional talk in their work lives, and the interpretive frames teachers use to understand and improve their own classroom practice.

— Marilyn Cochran-Smith and Susan L. Lytle,
"Research on Teaching and Teacher Research"

Teachers need to consider personal and career aspirations, including what kinds of knowledge and skills they want to acquire, when they are planning for professional development. Because learning is a career-long endeavor and a developmental process, learning to teach well is an integral aspect of professional development. Developing teaching expertise requires that teachers be knowledgeable about themselves, their students, the curriculum, and instructional practices, as well as the interactions among these factors in the classroom. To be effective, teachers must also engage in professional inquiry, studying the attributes of effective instruction, as well as making judgments about the effects of various learning techniques on their students. Proponents of professional development trust that, given a choice, teachers prefer to grow rather than stagnate. As they grow, teachers begin to believe that they can effect greater learning opportunities for students. Also, when teachers believe that they are personally responsible for their own growth and development, they tend to take it seriously.

Most of us have been on the receiving end of mandated, biannual, day-long inservice training. For many of us, it felt like a waste of time. Recalling these experiences brings back memories of teachers complaining, grading papers, and fidgeting. Few listened; even fewer brought back the ideas to their classrooms. Recently a group of teachers told me of a school system's attempt to encourage coaching. About 20 teachers from different schools within the district were wined and dined, assigned coaches, and informed that they were going to participate in coaching. Following a day of training, the teachers were instructed to coach six times and document their efforts.

Of the five teachers talking about it, one said she felt as if no one wanted her to be there, that she "was simply selected to participate because someone had to participate." Another said she tried it once but did not like it, nor did she trust the person with whom she was paired. Three said they did not participate and only pretended interest. All said they filled out the paperwork verifying that they had participated in coaching six times, when in actuality no one completed the process. Obviously coaching was not working.

Changing Dance Steps of Development

The process of collegial coaching as a means of developing and enhancing the professional talents of teachers requires that we think differently about the nature and function of professional development. Contemporary thinking emphasizes self-initiated development and emerging teacher leadership. Old ideas, like inservice education and staff development, are giving way to delivery systems that place teachers in greater control of the practices they choose to form and how they learn new ones. Ann Lieberman and Lynne Miller characterize self-direction of professional development as "growth-in-practice," a view of professional development that deems the study of practice intellectual, occurring through the study of theory and practice emanating from the job.[1] While growth-in-practice is important work for professional educators, collegial coaching is *growth-through-practice*, that is, developing talents in teaching through a process of studying instructional techniques and judgments away from the classroom delivery of instruction to students. *Growth-through-practice* means that classroom educators must engage in intellectual work and development of techniques and skills in various rehearsal situations—away from the classroom—in order to develop expertise in classroom performance. These rehearsal situations are safe environments whereby teachers can study their instructional actions and refine them prior to executing them in classroom instruction with students. Teachers study and learn about teaching free from the pressure of having to teach learners.

Inherent in the concept of *growth-through-practice* is the recognition that teaching talent is developed through reflective practice.[2] As teachers practice and reflect on their endeavors, they develop insights about their own teaching behaviors and the effects their instructional practices have on student learning. To grow in this way, teachers must have opportunities to study teaching continually, throughout the year, in rehearsal contexts and in their classrooms. I separate the study of teaching practices in rehearsal settings from delivering instruction to students in a classroom setting. When teachers study instructional practices away from their students, they can more aptly concentrate on instructional delivery without the concern of "having to teach" something. In doing so, instructional processes can be isolated and studied among caring professionals. As they engage in such inquiry, both on a personal level and in collaboration with other caring educators, learning about teaching becomes a process of experimentation, both personally and professionally.

> The inquiry process parallels the cycle of experiential learning. . . . Experience or practice provides the basis for reflection and analysis, which in turn informs future action. Thus, the assertion that teaching *is* inquiry. Engaging in research on one's own teaching and being reflexive about one's professional practice are one and the same when inquiry begins with and returns to the teaching self.[3]

While Ardra Cole and Gary Knowles speak of individual practice and inquiry, collegial coaching views individual practice and inquiry in concert with other caring educators. Thus, learning about teaching by engaging in collegial coaching rehearsals is a professional development dance with new steps.

Five new steps are introduced when thinking of professional development in terms of collegial coaching. The first requires teachers to back away from inservice training that tells them what they "ought" to be developing and advance toward opportunities where teachers can demonstrate and share their teaching talents with each other, developing insights about instruction that is effective for the school's learners. Of course, a safe environment is essential for teachers to talk about classroom practices—an activity that is the springboard for building shared school values and instructional practices.

The second step flows from the first: Administrators need to retreat from talking at teachers about their perceptions of needed instructional changes and progress toward talking with teachers about their concerns for improving instruction. As a consequence, teachers can take responsibility for designing practices that best impact their studies of teaching and learning.

The third step is to abandon mandated change in favor of that which is facilitated and mediated. While state- and district-mandated initiatives represent attempts to build public confidence in education, they may not (and most likely do not) address the individual professional needs of teachers. Likewise, teachers can always find ways to circumvent a mandate if they feel that it does not serve their interests.

Fourth, teachers must view self-study and inquiry about their instructional practices as the means for improving and refining instructional performance. Excellence in instructional delivery demands that classroom educators conduct research on the characteristics of effective instruction and the results of implementation of instruction to students. In so doing, the school is recreated as a learning environment in which theory emerges from practice and theory is studied as practice.

Finally, and most importantly, teacher development must distance itself from teacher evaluation. Confusing evaluation with improving teaching talent diminishes the results of both processes. Teacher evaluation is the measure of a teacher's effectiveness during classroom instruction. Teacher development is an ongoing, practice-oriented activity whereby teachers gain insights about teaching and learning processes. While evaluation is important in identifying teaching strengths and areas for development, in collegial coaching the responsibility for identifying these rests with the teacher, not the person observing the teacher. The teacher must perceive herself or himself as being in charge of making judgments about classroom performance.

Collegial coaching turns our attention toward the development of, rather than deficiencies in, teaching skills and talents. Teachers concentrate on the development of practices important to them in the delivery of effective instruction. It is a collaborative, reflective process in which teachers use inquiry and problem solving as methods for informing teaching practices. It is a nurturing process that enables teachers to integrate newly learned skills into their established repertoire of instructional practices through the support of other teachers. It is an empowering process that encourages and rewards professional growth. Finally, through collegial coaching, teachers come to believe that their professional development is intricately related to enhanced learning opportunities for themselves and their students.

Concepts about Development

Since John Dewey first began writing about how teachers develop, attempts to improve teaching expertise and foster teaching talent have been open for discussion. Often programs intended to improve teaching have emphasized skill development without taking into account the social, personal, and academic consequences of instructional practices. To develop expertise in teaching, Dewey stressed the importance of reflecting on practices and integrating observations into emerging theories of teaching and learning. He believed that as teachers study teaching and the impact of instruction on children, they become both the producers and consumers of knowledge about teaching. Likewise, James Nolan and Pam Francis point out that "teachers should be viewed as active constructors of their own knowledge about learning and teaching."[4]

Over the years, the process for developing teaching talent and expertise has evolved from something done to and for teachers to something done with and by teachers. The terms "inservice education," "staff development," and "professional development" have been used to describe the process. Each of these terms, as explained below, connotes assumptions about teachers and their development.

Inservice Education. In this most limited conceptualization of development, teachers are viewed as passive recipients of knowledge and skills. Others more knowledgeable about the needs of teachers—scholars and researchers—designate what it is teachers must learn and do in order to perform effectively in the classroom. Ann Lieberman and Lynne Miller define inservice as a variety of "teacher-proof" activities focused on technical skill development.[5] In their view, inservice education is synonymous with remedial education, implying a deficit model of teacher development. This idea of "fixing" teachers fosters the attitude that teachers are "passive recipients of someone else's knowledge . . . rather than sources of knowledge themselves or active participants in their own growth and development."[6]

For the most part, inservice education focuses on teaching some technical innovation or specific skill or technique deemed appropriate and planned for implementation in the classroom by someone else. It will be done almost mindlessly, since the emphasis is on implementing it rather than deliberating on its effect or helping teachers understand its use or implications. Examples of this are numerous: higher-order questioning methods, use of math manipulatives, and whole-language approaches. The application of instructional practices following inservice education was found to be nominal by Bruce Joyce and Beverly Showers.[7] In essence, inservice education conveys the message to teachers that they are not important; it is the implementation of the invention that is.

Staff Development. More encompassing of both teachers and school environments, staff development can be thought of as assistance in "adopting an externally designed program, making adaptations to some technological innovation, or implementing a federal or state program."[8] In this process, the elements of time and environment play important roles. It is assumed that teachers will acquire necessary knowledge and skills over time and connect their classroom practices to the school reorganization or improvement plan.

When teachers attempt to implement practices acquired through staff development, they most likely do so in the isolation of their own classrooms. Supervisors are the monitors and evaluators of progress. Evaluation is perceived as the means for assuring teaching competence. Little, if any, consideration is given to practicing the innovation or collaborating to attain competence. This is not to say that supervisors are not cognizant of the importance of practice, but they are often too busy with other duties to establish cooperative structures or find time in a densely packed school schedule for teachers to practice newly introduced programs. What results is a cycle of introduction to innovation followed by evaluation of teacher performance.

Inherent in both inservice education and staff development is a lack of ownership by teachers for the development and refinement of classroom practices. Teachers, caught in the introduction-evaluation cycle, tend to share the same values and beliefs about how to improve instruction as those designing and implementing the programs. That is, evaluation of their performance of the innovation in the classroom is evidence of teacher professional development. Internalization of the values inherent in the new practice is another matter and a secondary consideration.

While teachers may actively engage in the use of such practices, a nominal amount of time is spent by teachers studying their actions. If they attempt to incorporate new practices into their teaching repertoires, teachers do so because it is expected of them. Since classroom application and effects on student learning are analyzed and evaluated externally by supervisors or administrators, teachers often remain detached in their approach to learning new instructional practices. They, like their supervisors, perceive the exercise of the classroom practice and the evaluation of teaching performance as the means to developing their teaching talent. Again, they find themselves learning and doing things that others have directed them to do. Like robots, they go through the motions. They place little value on experimenting with instruction. The teacher's goal is to please the evaluator and to pass the evaluation.

Professional Development. This form of teacher growth differs considerably from inservice education and staff development. It is teacher sponsored and teacher driven. Teachers are responsible for determining, developing, and refining their own teaching practices. Each teacher works in an area of her or his own choosing. Evaluation of teacher performance is separated from the development process. Teacher development encourages teachers to engage in a dialogue about teaching that, in turn, informs teaching practices. Since teachers themselves determine what practices are to be developed or refined, they must commit to the study of their instructional practices and the effects these have on student learning.

Lieberman and Miller define teacher development "as continuous inquiry into practice."[9] In such a development process, teachers are not "objects of evaluation." They are "critical subjects" who have a direct and dynamic effect on shaping their talent and expertise in teaching.[10] Through continual study and experimentation with classroom instruction, teachers acquire dedication for taking charge of their own professional development and working together to improve learning for students. As Lieberman and Miller note,

> Teacher development involves teachers in learning about how to work together, how to make collective decisions, and how to structure continuous opportunities for their own growth. But at the same time, teachers must be constantly involved in new learning about students—their motivation, engagement, connection, and experience—through practicing new ways of teaching and providing for new ways of student learning. These two strands represent two distinct parts of teacher development, each part taking time, energy, and new knowledge.[11]

As teachers engage in collaborative activities to strengthen their talents and expertise, the responsibility for refining instructional practices is perceived by teachers as *inwardly* directed. It is not imposed on them by others in authority.

Using Dewey's ideas as the basis for his theories on coaching, Donald Schon refers to teachers who are participating in a developmental process as "reflective practitioners."[12] According to him, reflective practitioners use a "tacit knowledge base," or knowledge that is produced through practice and continual inquiry and analysis of one's actions, as a means for refining and evaluating one's instructional efforts. He defines this developmental activity as "reflective transformation of experience."[13]

Reflective transformation requires teachers to experiment with instructional practices in an attempt to create meaning out of problematic teaching situations through "problem setting" and "problem solving." "Problem setting is a process in which, interactively, we *name* the things to which we will attend and *frame* the context in which we will attend to them."[14] In other words, as teachers determine what aspects of their teaching they want to focus on developing within the context of their classroom instruction, they work through difficulties that may arise and refine instructional techniques. In this manner, teachers construct ideas and share beliefs and practices as they use their classroom experiences to inform future teaching acts as performing artists.

Using such a process of study, teachers engage in and develop teaching as an art form. "Teaching is an art . . . [that] is practiced as teachers struggle to adjust and readjust, to develop routines, and to establish patterns, only to recast what has been done in a new form to meet a new need or a new vision."[15] Like areas in the performing arts, such as acting and music, the instructional talents of teachers must be nurtured to be refined. The development of effective instructional practices that have appropriate technique and style is acquired through a process that integrates practice and reflection.

Professional development differs from inservice education and staff development in that teachers take the lead in initiating the direction, the process, and the outcomes of their study of teaching. When teachers are empowered, they are more likely to take charge of their development. Teachers know that it is their responsibility to refine their teaching performance. Teachers do so, not because someone else wants them to do things differently, but because they are entrusted to do so. In turn, teachers feel they are capable of doing things differently for the benefit of their students. This desire for improved classroom performance sets the stage for emerging teacher leadership.

Inservice education and staff development are necessary for introducing new innovations, techniques, and practices. However, in order to obtain competence in newly introduced instructional actions, teachers need extended opportunities to practice them in a safe environment before they can use them successfully with learners. Collegial coaching offers an opportunity for teachers to engage in the study of teaching and learning with respect for each other's personal and instructional aspirations.

Notes

1. Ann Lieberman and Lynne Miller, *Teachers Transforming Their World and Their Work* (New York: Teachers College Press, 1999), p. 59.

2. Donald A. Schon, *Educating the Reflective Practitioner: Toward a New Design for Teaching and Learning in the Professions* (San Francisco: Jossey-Bass, 1987).

3. Ardra L. Cole and J. Gary Knowles, *Researching Teaching: Exploring Teacher Development Through Reflexive Inquiry* (Boston: Allyn & Bacon, 2000), p. 94.

4. James Nolan and Pam Francis, "Changing Perspectives in Curriculum and Instruction," in *Supervision in Transition*, ed. Carl D. Glickman (Alexandria, Va.: Association for Supervision and Curriculum Development, 1992), p. 50.

5. Ann Lieberman and Lynne Miller, "Teacher Development in Professional Practice Schools," in *Professional Practice Schools: Linking Teacher Education and School Reform*, ed. Marsha Levine (New York: Teachers College Press, 1992), p. 105.

6. Ibid., p. 106.

7. Bruce Joyce and Beverly Showers, "Improving Inservice Training: The Messages of Research," *Educational Leadership* 37, no. 5 (1980): 379-85.

8. Lieberman and Miller, "Teacher Development," p. 106.

9. Ibid.

10. Paulo Freire, *The Politics of Education: Culture, Power, and Liberation* (South Hadley, Mass.: Bergin and Garvey, 1985).

11. Lieberman and Miller, "Teacher Development," pp. 120-21.

12. Schon, *Educating the Reflective Practitioner*. See also Donald A. Schon, *The Reflective Practitioner: How Professionals Think in Action* (New York: Basic Books, 1983).

13. Donald A. Schon, "Coaching Reflective Teaching," in *Reflection in Teacher Education*, ed. Peter P. Grimmett and Gaalen L. Erickson (New York: Teachers College Press, 1988), p. 25.

14. Schon, *The Reflective Practitioner*, p. 40, emphasis in the original.

15. Lieberman and Miller, "Teacher Development," p. 95.

CHAPTER THREE

Coaching for Professional Growth

Just as all teachers have different teaching styles, their learning styles are different. Teachers have options—they are in far greater control of their professional development than they ever were before.

— Bill Beaver
as quoted by John O'Neil in *ASCD Update*

The concept of coaching is inherent in different models of teacher development and referred to using different terms. Some of the more prevalent terms are "technical coaching," "challenge coaching," "team coaching," "peer assistance," "peer observation," "cognitive coaching," "peer coaching," and "collegial peer coaching."[1] Regardless of the name, proponents of coaching maintain that it is an ongoing process that assists in the broadening of teachers' instructional repertoires.

Beverly Showers defines coaching as "a process in which education professionals assist each other in negotiating the distance between acquiring new skills or teaching strategies and applying them skillfully and effectively in instruction."[2] Karolyn Snyder defines coaching as "a database technique that enables staff members to learn new skills, to modify practices, to solve problems together, and to develop basic skills."[3] This is coaching in its most technical sense. For both Showers and Snyder, the transfer of newly acquired skills is the goal of the coaching process.

Teachers can use the coaching process for many purposes. Showers has identified three goals of coaching: (1) build communities of teachers who continually engage in the study of their craft; (2) develop a shared language and set of common understandings necessary for the collegial study of new knowledge and skills; and, (3) provide a structure for follow-up to training for acquiring new teaching skills and strategies. The desire to use coaching as a development process emerges from a teacher's sense that something is not going as well as planned.

In coaching, teachers alternate between the roles of learner and development specialist as they work together to study instructional practices. By having another person with whom to share ideas, to observe, and to confer in solving instructional problems, teachers assemble a collegial learning culture that not only transforms the manner in which they teach, but also enhances their professional confidence. The bottom line in coaching is that teachers initiate the process and are responsible for the outcomes. In this manner, coaching is an empowering process that engages teachers in rediscovering themselves, the subject matter they teach, their students, and their classrooms.

Cognitive Coaching

The most widely known model of coaching, cognitive coaching, was conceived by Arthur Costa and Robert Garmston as a metacognitive, supervisory model.[4] Originally used by supervisors with teachers, cognitive coaching is intended to enhance teacher thinking and self-regulation of instruction. Costa and Garmston describe cognitive coaching as a supervisory strategy designed to enhance teachers' instructional perceptions, decisions, and cognitive processing.[5] They stress that it can be used by supervisors, principals, and peers. This coaching model has direct links with clinical supervision.[6] It is often a system-wide endeavor originating at the supervisory level of a school system and passed down through principals to teachers.

Peer Coaching

Peer coaching has emerged as a vehicle for teachers to collaborate on instructional issues and increase " professional talk."[7] It is a steadfast model of professional development to be used by and among teachers for the purpose of improving their instructional skills. Pamela Robbins defines peer coaching as "a confidential process through which two or more professional colleagues work together to reflect on current practices; expand, refine, and build new skills; share ideas; teach one another; conduct classroom research; or solve problems in the workplace."[8] Peer coaching is an on-site, continual process of professional development whereby teachers come together to solve problems and attain insights about instructional processes.[9]

Robbins maintains that the discussions and decisions that emerge from peer coaching should meet the needs of the coaching teachers and remain confidential.[10] Thus, peer coaching is not evaluation as it is presently perceived and conducted by schools. The source of the issues addressed in peer coaching is the self. Linda VanAssen and Saundra Tracey distinguish coaching from evaluation, noting that "the concept of collegial assistance emphasizes the assisting rather than the assessing nature of teachers helping teaching and removes the term 'supervision' and all its connotations."[11] Peer coaching must be clearly delineated and separated from the supervision and evaluation of teachers.

Collegial Coaching

As a model of professional growth, collegial coaching is an attempt to extend and refine peer coaching. It is implemented one on one, teacher by teacher, from the bottom up. It has evolved from ideas related to clinical supervision, teacher development, and artistic growth, and it blends concepts inherent in Dewey's and Schon's work on developing reflective practitioners in education.[12] The premises of collegial coaching are compatible with the idea that teachers are performing artists; like artists, they evolve and refine their techniques and styles throughout their careers by developing theories of teaching effectiveness based on practice and reflection on experience. Through this process, teachers expand their instructional repertoire.

Collegial coaching highlights the importance of the reflective process in teacher growth and development. It is a process of sharing, observing, practicing, reflecting, and conferring about instructional practice among colleagues. In his research on stages of teacher development, David Berliner posits that teachers grow and develop through reflection on practice.[13] It is this reflection that provides the means for teachers to become more cognizant of the relationships between teaching and learning.

The collegial coaching process emphasizes the collaborative development of teachers' instructional talents rather than the evaluation of teachers. It provides teachers opportunities to talk about instructional goals and practices in order to develop a shared vision about effective instruction. By collaborating, teachers "experience a heightened sense of teaching efficacy and professional empowerment. They become purposeful and enterprising in their actions. . . . [D]eveloping instructional practice becomes an important professional choice that motivates . . . teachers to become visionary about what can happen in teaching and in learning. In short, they take care of their professional lives and engage in perpetual learning about their craft."[14] The primary emphasis in collegial coaching is on refining teaching talent through reflective inquiry and collaboration with others who teach.

Notes

1. For information on technical coaching, see Robert Garmston, "How Administrators Support Peer Coaching," *Educational Leadership* 44, no. 2 (1987): 19-26; see also Bruce Joyce and Beverly Showers, "The Coaching of Teaching," *Educational Leadership* 40, no. 1 (1982): 4-8, 10. For information about challenge coaching, see Garmston, "How Administrators Support Peer Coaching." For team coaching, see Kenneth Moffett, Jane St. John, and Joann Isken, "Training and Coaching Beginning Teachers: An Antidote to Reality Shock," *Educational Leadership* 44, no. 2 (1987): 34-36. Information about peer assistance appears in Susan James, Daniel Heller, and William Ellis, "Peer Assistance in a Small District: Windham Southeast, Vermont," in *Supervision in Transition*, ed. Carl D. Glickman (Alexandria, Va.: Association for Supervision and Curriculum Development, 1992), pp. 97-111. The topic of peer observation is treated in Joy Anastos and Robert Ancowitz, "A Teacher-Directed Peer Coaching Project," *Educational Leadership* 44, no. 3 (1987): 40-42. For information on cognitive coaching, see Arthur L. Costa and Robert Garmston, "Coaching Elegance" (paper presented at the annual meeting of the Association for Supervision and Curriculum Development, New Orleans, April 1992). For information on peer coaching, see Bruce S. Cooper, John E. Iorio, and John Poster, "Organizing Schools for Teacher Collegiality: The New York City Experience," *Education* 111, no. 1 (1990): 68-76; Marylou Dantonio, *Teachers Coaching Teachers: Instructional Leadership through Empowering Teachers* (Bloomington, Ind.: Phi Delta Kappa, 1988), p. 6; Marylou Dantonio, *Teacher Professionalism and Leadership in Louisiana: A Resource Manual* (Baton Rouge, La.: Louisiana Department of Education, 1992); Cynthia

G. Desrochers and Sheryll R. Klein, "Teacher-Directed Peer Coaching as a Follow-up to Staff Development," *Journal of Staff Development* 11, no. 2 (1990): 6-10; and Pamela Robbins, *How to Plan and Implement a Peer Coaching Program* (Alexandria, Va.: Association for Supervision and Curriculum Development, 1991), p. 1. For information on collegial peer coaching, see Dantonio, *Teacher Professionalism and Leadership in Louisiana* and Garmston, "How Administrators Support Peer Coaching."

2. Beverly Showers, "Teachers Coaching Teachers," *Education Leadership* 42, no. 7 (1985): 48.

3. Karolyn J. Snyder, "Schooling Transformation: The Context for Professional Coaching and Problem Solving," in *Clinical Supervision: Coaching for Higher Performance*, ed. Robert H. Anderson and Karolyn J. Snyder (Lancaster, Penn.: Technomic Publishing Company, 1993), p. 32.

4. Arthur L. Costa and Robert Garmston, "The Art of Cognitive Coaching: Supervision for Intelligent Teaching," (training syllabus of the Institute for Intelligent Behavior, Sacramento, Cal., 1990).

5. Costa and Garmston, "Coaching Elegance."

6. Anderson and Snyder, *Clinical Supervision*.

7. Judith W. Little, "Norms of Collegiality and Experimentation: Workplace Conditions of School Success," *American Educational Research Journal* 19, no. 3 (1982): 325-40.

8. Robbins, *How to Plan and Implement a Peer Coaching Program*, p. 1.

9. Dantonio, *Teacher Professionalism and Leadership in Louisiana*.

10. Robbins, *How to Plan and Implement a Peer Coaching Program*. See also Dantonio, *Teacher Professionalism and Leadership in Louisiana* and Dantonio, *Teachers Coaching Teachers*.

11. Linda A. VanAssen and Saundra J. Tracy, "Using What We Know about Collegial Assistance," *Journal of Staff Development* 12, no. 4 (1991): 48.

12. For information about clinical supervision, see Anderson and Snyder, Clinical Supervision; for teacher training, see Bruce Joyce and Beverly Showers, *Student Achievement through Staff Development* (New York: Longman, 1988).

13. David C. Berliner, "The Development of Expertise in Pedagogy" (Charles W. Hunt Memorial Lecture presented at the annual meeting of the American Association for Colleges of Teacher Education, New Orleans, February 1988).

14. Peter P. Grimmett, Olaf P. Rostad, and Blake Ford, "The Transformation of Supervision," in *Supervision in Transition*, ed. Carl D. Glickman (Washington D. C.: Association for Supervision and Curriculum Development, 1992), p. 186.

CHAPTER FOUR

Outcomes of Collegial Coaching

The emptiness of teachers' professional growth tends to become a numb ache felt in students' learning opportunities.
— Susan Rosenholtz,
Teachers' Workplace: The Social Organization of Schools

The goal of teacher development, according to Susan Rosenholtz, is to improve instructional effectiveness, that is, to increase learning for students.[1] Assumptions about how teachers develop and what is important in their development influence the kinds of learning opportunities school districts afford teachers. As previously noted, the latitude and autonomy administrators yield to teachers to determine professional development issues and engage in collegial coaching are likely to pay off in student achievement.

Collegial coaching facilitates teachers' studies of teaching practices. In their reflections on classroom experiences and through different types of collegial study groups where they can focus on excellence in delivery, teachers can attain a sense of efficacy or certainty about their instructional practices by concentrating on precision in instructional delivery. Working together, they can create a collaborative work environment conducive to developing shared goals. In turn, collaboration diminishes the barriers of isolation that impede sharing. How teachers think and feel about their instructional efforts and the extent to which they collaborate impact not only their development but also student learning.[2] It is important to remember that the focus of collegial coaching is on the reflection and study of teaching practices to refine those practices. It is not centered on the deficiencies in teaching practices. By engaging in the process of collegial coaching, teachers can practice and refine techniques to enhance instructional delivery. By inquiring into teaching, teachers are better prepared to carry out informed decisions about instructional delivery.

Frames of Knowing

In order to foster teaching expertise, the teacher must be an active participant in determining what aspect of her or his teaching will be addressed, how it will be addressed, and how it will be assessed. Thus, teachers develop frames of knowing about instructional practices. These are the cornerstones for developing theories about instructional delivery that are grounded in practice. It is through the study of practice that teachers become conscious and insightful about the effects particular instructional techniques have on student learning. In turn, teachers give voice to tacit theories as to why a particular practice works with some students and not with others. Viewing learning in context, teachers apply their theories about how students learn through their delivery of instruction.

Michael Connelly and Jean Clandinin refer to frames of knowing as "personal practical knowledge."[3] It is a phrase that captures the role experience plays in developing theories about classroom practice. In other words, what teachers experience and how they experience it formulate their understanding of the teaching and learning processes. Mary Kennedy describes the process of attaining knowledge about teaching as developing "expertise in deliberate action."[4] Deliberate action is doing what we intend. Kennedy says that effective instruction is based on the intricacies of what teachers intend to do in the classroom, how they analyze the process and results, and how they make adaptations based on what they discover as they deliver instruction. According to her, "Deliberate actions are based in experience, and expertise in deliberate action is most likely to be developed by experience in deliberating; that is, experience in establishing real goals in real situations, working toward those goals, and learning from these experiences which goals can and can't be met in which kinds of circumstances."[5]

To instruct with *deliberate actions* requires that we prepare for our instruction with students. This means we must invent safe practice sessions that allow us to investigate our assumptions, beliefs, and values about teaching and learning and refine our techniques and strategies by rehearsing them and analyzing them with other educators who care. Such rehearsing becomes a part of our experiences in learning about teaching. In turn, our inquiry into teaching through collegial study groups enriches our understanding of specific instructional techniques and processes. Thus, we become more thoughtful educators. Max Van Manen suggests that we must constantly learn from our experiences, converse collaboratively about them, play out our learning, and revise our understanding of teaching and learning though inquiry.[6] Collegial practice of instructional actions outside our classroom performances permits us to inquire with greater concentration about how we deliver instruction, and it refines our aptitude to deliver quality instruction to students.

Stages of Professional Development for Teachers

At the heart of professional development is the issue of how teachers best develop instructional talents and become knowledgeable and deliberate in the delivery of instruction. The attributes of teacher professional development have been identified through expert-novice research.[7] These investigations reveal that the transition from novice to expert teacher is dependent on time and experience. Terry Wildman and Jerome Niles note that professional growth is an emerging quality that matures over time in specific and predictable patterns.[8] In terms of planning and conducting lessons, novice teachers' content knowledge is less elaborate, structured, and accessible than expert teachers', resulting in disconnected, incomplete lessons. As teachers attain experience and have opportunities to gain expertise, they develop more elaborate structures of content knowledge that facilitate the delivery of lessons that are cohesive, connected, and related to prior learning.[9]

The importance of expert-novice research is that teacher educators have begun to hone in on the attributes contributing to degrees of expertise. David Berliner has identified five specific stages of teacher development that are not necessarily hierarchical, nor can they be attributed to years of service. Not all teachers develop into experts, Berliner points out, and some beginning teachers are more expert than teachers who have taught for 20 years.

The five teacher development stages identified by Berliner are (1) novice, (2) advance beginner, (3) competent, (4) proficient, and (5) expert. Berliner attributes experience as a key factor in distinguishing the novice from the expert teacher. More importantly, his work reveals the significance of reflection on practice as the means through which teachers evolve a conceptual schema about teaching. Berliner found that expert teachers have well-established classroom routines that permit them to make fairly accurate predictions about students and classroom events. Novice teachers, lacking experience, are not sophisticated in their abilities to predict instructional events and problems.

Likewise, in her study of teacher decision making during planning, teaching, and reflection on instruction, Delores Westerman found that expert teachers differed from novice teachers in the extent to which they were able to see causal relationships between teaching actions and learner behaviors.[10] The novices "usually blamed the students for bad behavior without giving any underlying reasons for their actions"[11]; expert teachers provided reasonable explanations for student behaviors, linking teaching action with desirable or undesirable student behavior.

In a study of the planning and teaching practices of mathematics teachers, Gaea Leinhardt found that teachers' classroom practices are influenced by knowledge of the subject, pedagogical theory, the class agenda, and knowledge of students.[12] In this and other studies, expert teachers more readily utilized information about students and were more sensitive to student questions in planning and conducting lessons than were novice teachers. The investigators concluded that expert teachers possess more elaborate constructs of instruction than novice teachers do. In another study of experienced and novice English teachers, experienced teachers integrated their knowledge of students' backgrounds in planning and conducting lessons.[13] Novice teachers were more apt to plan content without regard for student background or interests.

Expert teachers, regardless of their years of service, have a vast and rich experiential base to draw on as they continue their journey to develop teaching talent and to understand the effects of instructional practices on student learning. Obviously, novice teachers need more time, guidance, and direction in thinking through their experiences in order to develop sophistication in understanding the complex relationships involved in the instructional process. However, both expert and novice teachers can benefit greatly from the use of a collegial coaching process to enhance teaching talent. Through sharing and reflecting on instructional practices, all teachers have greater opportunities to ascertain the best practices to use in specific educational contexts.

Collegial coaching offers teachers occasions to reflect, study, and deliberate on instructional experiences. In doing so, they develop frames of knowing about instruction that contribute to the enhancement of their classroom performance. By collaborating, teachers are afforded opportunities to attain insights into effective practices, building knowledge and confidence in delivering effective instruction for students. And finally, collegial coaching is a synergistic process that breathes life into a school climate, filling it with dynamic, interactive dialogues about instruction.

Notes

1. Susan J. Rosenholtz, *Teachers' Workplace: The Social Organization of Schools* (New York: Longman, 1989).

2. John Dewey, *Experience and Education* (New York: Macmillan, 1938); Karen F. Osterman, "Reflective Practice: A New Agenda for Education," *Education and Urban Society* 22, no. 2 (1990): 132-52; Donald A. Schon, *Educating the Reflective Practitioner: Toward a New Design for Teaching and Learning in the Professions* (San Francisco: Jossey-Bass, 1987); Max Van Manen, "Linking Ways of Knowing with Ways of Being Practical," *Curriculum Inquiry* 6, no. 3 (1977): 205-28; Patricia T. Ashton, "Teacher Efficacy: A Motivational Paradigm for Effective Teacher Education," *Journal of Teacher Education* 35, no. 5 (1984): 28-32; Albert Bandura, "Self-Efficacy: Toward a Unifying Theory of Behavioral Change," *Psychological Review* 84, no. 2 (1977): 191-215; and Thomas R. Guskey, "Context Variables That Affect Measures of Teacher Efficacy," *Journal of Educational Research* 81, no. 1 (1987): 41-47.

3. F. Michael Connelly and D. Jean Clandinin, *Teachers As Curriculum Planners: Narratives of Experience* (New York: Teachers College Press, 1988).

4. Mary M. Kennedy, "Establishing Professional Schools for Teachers," in *Professional Practice Schools: Linking Teacher Education and School Reform*, ed. Marsha Levine (New York: Teachers College Press, 1992), pp. 63-80.

5. Ibid., p. 70.

6. Max Van Manen, *Researching Lived Experience: Human Science for an Action Sensitive Pedagogy* (Albany, NY: State University of New York Press, 1990).

7. David C. Berliner, "The Development of Expertise in Pedagogy" (Charles W. Hunt Memorial Lecture presented at the annual meeting of the American Association for Colleges of Teacher Education, New Orleans, February 1988); Marylou Dantonio and James Randels, "Differences in Pedagogical Thought Processes Used in Planning, Conducting, and Reflecting by Novice and Experienced English Teachers" (paper presented at the annual conference of the Association of Teacher Educators, New Orleans, February 1991); Gaea Leinhardt and Ralph T. Putnam, "Profile of Expertise in Elementary School Mathematics Teaching," *Arithmetic Teacher* 34, no. 2 (1986): 8-29; Carol Livingston and Hilda

Borko, "Expert-Novice Differences in Teaching: A Cognitive Analysis and Implications for Teacher Education," *Journal of Teacher Education* 40, no. 4 (1989): 36-42; Delores A. Westerman, "Expert and Novice Teacher Decision Making," *Journal of Teacher Education* 42, no. 4 (1991): 292-305; Terry M. Wildman and Jerome A. Niles, "Reflective Teachers: Tensions between Abstractions and Realities," *Journal of Teacher Education* 38, no. 4 (1987): 25-31.

8. Wildman and Niles, "Reflective Teachers."

9. Hilda Borko and Carol Livingston, "Cognition and Improvisation: Differences in Mathematics Instruction by Expert and Novice Teachers," *American Educational Research Journal* 26, no. 4 (1989): 473-98; Gaea Leinhardt, *Novice and Expert Knowledge of Individual Student's Achievement*, a report of research conducted by the Pennsylvania Learning Research and Development Center, University of Pittsburgh, for the National Institute of Education, Washington, D.C., 1983, ERIC No. ED 233 985; Leinhardt and Putnam, "Profile of Expertise"; Westerman, "Expert and Novice Teacher Decision Making."

10. Westerman, "Expert and Novice Teacher Decision Making."

11. Ibid., p. 12.

12. Gaea Leinhardt, *Novice and Expert Knowledge of Individual Student's Achievement*; Gaea Leinhardt, "Math Lessons: A Contrast of Novice and Expert Competence," *Journal for Research in Mathematics Education* 20, no. 1 (1989): 52-75; see also Borko and Livingston, "Cognition and Improvisation."

13. Dantonio and Randels, "Differences in Pedagogical Thought Processes."

CHAPTER FIVE

The Cycle of Collegial Coaching

The magic is not in the wand. It is in the magician.
— Barbara Turner,
"Accelerated Schools' Successes"

Collegial coaching, as a form of continual, on-site faculty development, provides the impetus for self-direction in professional development. Teachers who have been using this process often remark that it is "magical."[1] By magical, they mean that their ideas about developing teaching talent have changed from something they do because it is expected of them to something they do because it fosters positive feelings about their efforts in the classroom and their work with other teachers. As they work through the phases of collegial coaching, teachers can be transformed from those who consume knowledge about teaching into those who construct and use teaching knowledge gleaned through their reflection on instruction.

Collegial coaching borrows its structure from Robert Anderson and Karolyn Snyder's clinical supervision process with two major differences: teachers' perceptions of the purpose of observation and the inclusion of reflection time.[2] In clinical supervision, the supervisor or principal is usually responsible for providing feedback to a teacher about classroom performance. The teacher interprets the feedback and need to change a practice as being externally directed; the supervisor, not the teacher, designates the need for change. The teacher thinks, "What is it that my supervisor wants me to change?" or "What does my supervisor think about my lesson?" In collegial coaching, however, the teacher thinks, "What do I want to focus on in developing my instructional practices?" and "How do I go about getting the help I need to improve my teaching?"

In collegial coaching, it is the teacher being coached who must make decisions about what instructional practices will be changed. Effective instructional practices emerge from interactions with a trusted colleague following time to reflect. The teacher must perceive that the trusted colleague is competent in the instructional area the teacher desires to improve. As teachers participate in the coaching process, they become partners in the study of teaching. Prior to conferring with each other, time is provided for individual reflection. In conferring with each other, the coaching partners discern discrepancies between what the coached teacher intended to do in a lesson and her or his actual classroom performance. Their deliberations result in a more complete understanding and internalization of instructional processes in relationship to the classroom context.

Phases of the Cycle

There are four major phases to the collegial coaching cycle. Each has a specific purpose that is described briefly in this section. A more detailed account of the procedures and questions for each phase of the cycle is provided in the next section. Depending on the amount of time available and their goals, teachers may choose to concentrate on one or all of the phases of the collegial coaching cycle. These are:

- planning,
- observation of the teaching performance,
- reflection time, and
- debriefing.

Planning. This is the most important phase of the cycle, since it is here that the teacher and coach frame the "problem focus" of the lesson.[3] Here they discuss the teacher's purposes for the lesson, specify and sequence the instructional events, identify problems that may arise in delivery, and determine strategies for dealing with the anticipated problems. In terms of students, the coach assists the teacher in specifying on- and off-task behaviors. Planning is concluded as the teacher and coach make decisions about what specifically is to be observed by the coach during lesson implementation, as well as how data will be collected so that it is useful to the teacher in making decisions concerning the effectiveness of the lesson.

Planning presents an opportunity for the coached teacher to vocalize, play out, and run through all of the events of the lesson. In actors' language, it is a dress rehearsal; in linebackers' language, it is a scrimmage. It offers the coaching partners time to think through, picture, and understand the teacher's lesson plan. They clarify and extend the teacher's expectations for the delivery of the lesson. As the coaching partners converse, they determine what will take place by developing a common vocabulary to describe the events of the lesson. The framing of the lesson and discussions about what to observe and how to observe it are done so that the coaching partners can experience the lesson with a consistent mental picture about what is to take place during the teacher's classroom delivery of the instructional plan.

Observation of the Teaching Performance. During this phase, the coach observes the instructional or learning behaviors specified during the planning phase. The coach records information related to the observation focus using data collection procedures and instruments agreed upon during planning. The observation instrument is not an evaluation check list. The coach focuses on only the specific behaviors identified in the planning phase.

In recording observations of the teaching performance, every effort is made by the coach to portray the events of the unfolding lesson as accurately and objectively as possible. The coach avoids making inferences and judgments about her or his observations. In recording the specific events of the teaching performance, the coach is the teacher's eyes. The coach's notes become a mirror that can assist the teacher in seeing more clearly what was taking place while she or he was involved in teaching.

Reflection Time. Following the observation, both teacher and coach spend time alone reflecting on the teaching performance. Reflection time is necessary for the coaching partners to ascertain insights about the performance, and it is critical to the development of teaching talent. Through reflection on instructional actions, teachers discover important relationships between their teaching behaviors and student learning. Reflection time helps the coaching partners hone in on what the teacher needs to do differently. For the teacher, reflection time provides a chance to devise solutions to problems and determine what assistance is needed from the coach.

Debriefing. Here the coaching partners share their insights and begin a problem-solving process to effect changes in the coached teacher's instructional practices. The focus of the debriefing phase is on discrepancies between what the teacher pictured or visualized would happen when preparing for instruction compared to what actually occurred while teaching the lesson. It is the identification and understanding of these discrepancies that motivate the desire for change in a teacher's instructional repertoire.

Throughout this discussion, the coaching partners share their perceptions and find solutions to problematic situations. As a result of this professional dialogue, the coached teacher has information that can be used to effect changes in her or his instructional practices. One goal of collegial coaching is for teachers to become more expert in the delivery of instruction. During the debriefing conference, the coaching partners problem solve about instructional practices as well as detect specific contextual aspects of effective instructional delivery.

Effects of the Cycle on Teachers

The collegial coaching process fosters the outcomes deemed important in teacher professional development. First, through dialogue between and among teachers, a peer vision or common understanding of the expectations of the teaching-learning event evolves. This peer vision assists in facilitating common school goals and teamwork among teachers. Second, through continual reflection on the discrepancies between planned instruction and executed instruction, each teacher develops a self-vision that informs her or his experience and pedagogical knowledge. This self-vision has a powerful influence on a teacher's sense of efficacy and is instrumental in bridging gaps between theory and practice. It provides the impetus for understanding teaching as problem focusing rather than problem hiding. And third, as teachers work together they begin to feel a sense of camaraderie that facilitates emerging leadership. This camaraderie has a magical quality that lays the foundation for initiating and sustaining a professional school culture committed to the study of teaching and learning.

As the phases of collegial coaching are carried out, the coaching partners engage in a self-initiated development process that acts as a catalyst for emerging teacher leadership. Teacher leadership manifests itself as teachers form collegial bonds that contribute to their desires to sponsor and guide the professional development of other teachers. However, it is important to remember that it is the teacher, not the coach, who controls what talents she or he wants to refine and how these will be developed. As a result, teachers are responsible for their own development plan. They own it. Therefore, they are more likely to carry it out.

Notes

1. Marylou Dantonio, *Teacher Professionalism and Leadership in Louisiana: A Resource Manual* (Baton Rouge, La.: Louisiana Department of Education, 1992).

2. Robert H. Anderson and Karolyn J. Snyder, eds., *Clinical Supervision: Coaching for Higher Performance* (Lancaster, Penn.: Technomic Publishing, 1993).

3. Donald A. Schon, *Educating the Reflective Practitioner: Toward a New Design for Teaching and Learning in the Professions* (San Francisco: Jossey-Bass, 1987).

CHAPTER SIX

The Collegial
School Environment

If we can create schools that excite both teachers and students and provide the conditions that improve the quality of teaching, we will do much to create schools that genuinely educate.

— Eliot Eisner,
"Why Standards May Not Improve Schools"

Establishing a successful collegial coaching program may require that the school culture be rethought. Collegial coaching cannot be implemented in a school environment hostile to its philosophy. Bureaucratic, hierarchical models of program delivery need to be transformed into "communitarian" ones that encourage the safe sharing of instructional purposes and values, stories about teaching successes and failures, classroom and school rituals, and lesson artifacts important to the learning environment.[1] In such an environment, collegiality among teachers and administrators is the norm. School administrators believe that teachers are capable of instructional leadership, and they value teachers as instructional leaders. As with any change that occurs in schools, attention must be paid to what is worth doing and why it is done.[2]

In a collegial school culture, educators regard collective inquiry and experimentation with instruction as evidence of school improvement. Collegial interaction is an important factor in teacher growth.[3] Implementing processes that encourage teacher communication about instructional practices can provide the foundation for emerging teacher leadership. Teachers perceiving themselves as leaders can revitalize the school community and establish a nurturing, engaging environment for teacher learning. By framing teacher learning as a process of collaboration, teachers have the opportunity to engage in instructional development, viewing learning to teach as cumulative and contextual.

Terrence Deal and Kent Peterson note that an engaging, collaborative culture has a powerful effect on a school community. It is the culture of a school that affects the success of student learning. According to these authors, productive school cultures impact school renewal in the following ways:

- Culture fosters school effectiveness and productivity.
- Culture improves collegial and collaborative activities that foster better communication and problem-solving practices.
- Culture fosters successful change and improvement efforts.

- Culture builds commitment and identification of staff, students, and administrators.
- Culture amplifies the energy, motivation, and vitality of a school staff, students, and community.
- Culture increases the focus of daily behavior and attention on what is important and valued.[4]

It is important that all educators within the school community understand, accept, and value communal inquiry as a condition for establishing a sound school culture. To engage in communal development and leadership, teachers need a climate of trust and support that facilitates breaking down barriers. Most important is the manner in which teachers are encouraged to collaborate and inquire about instructional issues. They should feel free and be free to interact with each other without the threat of evaluation. Experimentation with instructional practices can flourish in an atmosphere unguarded by the fear of evaluation. In addition, a community of educators who engage in the study of teaching practices and the development of teaching talent cannot be mandated by administrators. It develops from the bottom up, teacher by teacher, with continued nurturance and support from administrators.

When teachers work with each other as colleagues to inform and improve instructional practices, the process is both relational and collegial. Collegial coaching is a reciprocal, one-on-one, person-to-person communication process about the effects of instruction on learners. Collegiality is fostered as teachers share ideas and collaborate to improve instructional practices. By collaborating, they can form a support network of trusted colleagues. Both colleagueship and collaboration are necessary ingredients for teachers to rethink their roles, participate in studying instructional processes, and perceive their professional development as part of their daily work in schools.[5]

By collaboratively engaging in the study of teaching, teachers can have greater influence on each other's teaching behaviors through the use of problem solving. They can begin to view teaching as "problem focused."[6] When teachers perceive teaching as such, their reluctance to experiment with instructional practices is usually dispelled. Through continual inquiry into instructional practice, teachers can develop a greater sense and understanding of how learning takes place for students. Concomitantly, learning opportunities for children are enhanced. In her study of teachers' workplaces, Susan Rosenholtz found that the more opportunities teachers had to learn, the higher their students' performance was in basic skills.[7]

Additionally, as teachers coach each other, they can create a synergism that nourishes their self-esteem, enabling them to feel more control over their own professional development. As teachers become more confident in the delivery of instruction, they often reach out to other teachers, exploring opportunities for productive participation in instructional leadership. As a result, collegial coaching can influence teachers' desires to collaborate, develop a shared vision about instruction, and engage in collective and shared leadership. As Rosenholtz notes, "Teacher collaboration is the final predictor of teachers' learning opportunities. Learning may be the direct outcome of collaboration as teachers request from and offer colleagues new ideas, strategies, and techniques. But quite apart from the rendering of technical assistance, collaboration may indirectly influence learning through the leadership of teachers within the school. Teacher leaders' enthusiasm for experimentation . . . has a contagious quality. The pedagogical appeal of such energetic locomotion seems almost irresistible in inducing others to share, to experiment, and to grow."[8]

Collegial coaching places teachers at the heart of their own development. Even though the principal is the catalyst for change, teachers are the key players in instigating it. Improved learning opportunities for students rely on developing the instructional talents of teachers. Therefore, attention to the development of teaching talents must be given the same effort afforded student learning.[9] Most importantly, as teachers develop expertise and experience success with collegial coaching, they can begin to believe in themselves as instructional leaders capable of contributing to the development of teaching talent in other teachers.

Notes

1. Catherine A. Lugg and William L. Boyd, "Leadership for Collaboration: Reducing Risk and Fostering Resilience," *Phi Delta Kappan* 75, no. 3 (1993): 253-58.

2. Martin L. Maehr and Stephanie A. Parker, "A Tale of Two Schools—and the Primary Task of Leadership," *Phi Delta Kappan* 75, no. 3 (1993): 233-39.

3. Ann Lieberman and Lynne Miller, "Teacher Development in Professional Practice Schools," in *Professional Practice Schools: Linking Teacher Education and School Reform*, ed. Marsha Levine (New York: Teachers College Press, 1992); Susan J. Rosenholtz, *Teachers' Workplace: The Social Organization of Schools* (New York: Longman, 1989); Pamela Robbins, *How to Plan and Implement a Peer Coaching Program* (Alexandria, Va.: Association for Supervision and Curriculum Development, 1991).

4. Terrence Deal and Kent D. Peterson, *Shaping School Culture: The Heart of Leadership* (San Francisco: Jossey-Bass, 1999), pp. 7-8.

5. Lieberman and Miller, "Teacher Development in Professional Practice Schools"; Rosenholtz, *Teachers' Workplace*.

6. Donald A. Schon, *Educating the Reflective Practitioner: Toward a New Design for Teaching and Learning in the Professions* (San Francisco: Jossey-Bass, 1987).

7. Rosenholtz, *Teachers' Workplace*.

8. Ibid., p. 79.

9. Mary M. Kennedy, "Establishing Professional Schools for Teachers," in *Professional Practice Schools: Linking Teacher Education and School Reform*, ed. Marsha Levine (New York: Teachers College Press, 1992).

CHAPTER SEVEN

Distinguishing Collegial Professional Development From Supervision and Evaluation

[T]raditional forms of supervision are being questioned; newer avenues to teacher growth are more peer oriented and less likely to fit comfortably under the mantle of supervision.

— John O'Neil,
"Supervision Reappraised"

The mantle of supervision that John O'Neil refers to is slow to change. In its current state, it is also incongruous with the needs of many school staff members. In this chapter we explore the current mantle of supervision and describe a new, collegial mantle that encourages professional learning as a framework for supervision, evaluation, and professional development.

Most schools today operate in a top-down, hierarchical, supervisory model. This organizational structure can be represented by an isosceles triangle. At the top is the principal, the center point of the school. The principal is responsible for and makes all decisions affecting the education of students. At the base of the triangle are the teachers. Their classroom performance and professional development are measured by evaluations conducted by the center point, the principal. From this perspective, professional development is seen as something that is evaluated with little attention paid to ways teachers evolve expertise in the practice of teaching.

In a top-down model, professional development is perceived by teachers as externally directed: The impetus for instructional improvement is designated by someone with authority over teachers. Teachers conform to the vision and expectations of the designated leader of the school—the principal or the principal's appointee. "Within this type of evaluation, teachers are viewed as deficient, and their personal knowledge is ignored."[1] Needless to say, they have little involvement in their own professional development, other than being subjects under investigation in the evaluative process.

Hierarchical, one-way communication dominates the current evaluation model. This hierarchical construct is limiting, and it may damage teachers' self-esteem. It stifles avenues for teachers to reflect on instructional practices and to make sense of teaching and learning. It is a means of managing continual professional learning and school improvement.[2] In such a context, any kind of development activity can be a demeaning experience, because teachers have little, if any, impact on their own professional growth, and administrators may be at odds with teachers about what their professional development should entail. In fact, a hierarchical, supervisory school atmosphere conflicts directly with the idea that teachers are both the consumers and producers of knowledge about teaching. It negates the role reflection plays in the development of teaching talent. It ignores the necessity of teacher self-study as a means for investigating student learning and sustaining the school as a learning organization. Likewise, such a school climate is antithetical to establishing sound collegial relationships and collective teaming that heighten opportunities for shared leadership as a means for improving the education of students.

The new collegial mantle we propose regards teacher development, supervision, and evaluation as separate processes. Teacher development is the refinement and enhancement of teaching talent. It is teacher sponsored and teacher driven through processes such as collegial coaching. It relies on continual inquiry to improve teaching practices.[3] It is a collaborative process whereby school staff share ideas and successful practices, solve instructional problems, and celebrate teaching and learning. It honors teachers as learners. It assumes teachers grow through their study of instructional contexts. Ann Lieberman and Lynn Miller write, "[T]eaching is intellectual work and . . . professional development occurs when teachers have the opportunity to learn from theory and practice as part of their jobs."[4]

While we advocate for a collegial process of development, we are most cognizant of Martin Huberman's caution that a collegial climate can create a culture for discussion without actually changing classroom practice or influencing teachers' beliefs and knowledge.[5] To change classroom practice is not easily accomplished. Because teaching is a performing art, sound professional development must provide ways for professional practitioners to confront themselves as learners and contend with the beliefs they hold about teaching and learning and how professional growth occurs.[6]

For teachers to develop insightful knowledge about teaching and learning and to evolve artful, skillful practices appropriate to quality instruction, they must challenge their beliefs and knowledge, as well as develop a repertoire of methodologies. Professional development requires that professional educators continually challenge their practice. They must be provided with opportunities to think, read, and reflect vigorously about learning and about their teaching performances. Teachers must have rigorous sessions to develop habits of practice in order to refine their instructional delivery. As teachers carry out their understandings in classroom practice, they must be capable of thinking reflectively about the relationships between theory and practice so they can derive new understandings, issues, and problems concerning students, curriculum, and the teaching/learning processes.[7]

The development process described above is inconsistent with current school-based supervisory or evaluative practices. For the most part, it does not exist.[8] In place of teacher development, school organizations supervise and evaluate teachers. Theoretically, supervision is aligned with teacher development. It involves both teachers and supervisors attaining common understandings of the relationship between teaching practices and student learning and the effects their practices have on learning.[9] In practice, however, supervision governs the impact of instruction as it conforms to district or school goals and programs. Its influence is on coordination, not individual or team development. It is not teacher sponsored or teacher driven. It does not require teachers to grapple with issues of teaching and learning. Thus, it is not surprising that educational "experts have long contended that brief, episodic supervisory encounters [for the purpose of evaluation] . . . do little to promote teacher growth."[10]

Evaluation is the assessment of instructional delivery "for the purpose of making personnel decisions and determining contractual renewal, merit pay, assignments, and placements on career ladders."[11] The outcome of evaluation is the perspective of the evaluator, most likely using an observation/evaluative instrument designed to collect universal data about instruction. The collection instruments are designed to make judgements about teachers and their instructional performance.

Evaluation today is clinical in nature, requiring the evaluator to obtain information about a teacher's lesson prior to the observation. This is usually done briefly, before the class is observed, or by reviewing the teacher's lesson plan. After the observation, the evaluator meets with the teacher to relate his/her observations and judgments. The teacher responds and signs. When evaluation consists solely of isolated observations without collegial interaction, the potential for professional growth stops. Evaluation, like supervision, is necessary and important; it is not a development process.

There are several problems with the current mantle of supervision operating as a system for teacher evaluation. It cannot serve as a process of development, since the processes and ends of each are different. According to Charlotte Danielson, "[M]any of the evaluation systems in use today were developed in the early 1970s and reflect what educators believed at the time."[12] Likewise, a myriad of practitioners' perspectives regarding the current state of teacher evaluation identify the following weaknesses.

The processes of clinical supervision and teacher development are incongruent. Most studies of clinical supervision fail to demonstrate a relationship between evaluation and improved classroom performance.[13] In practice, evaluations are often snapshots in time, capturing only the moment of instruction during the administrator's scheduled observation. Thus, the supervisor's evaluation often is based upon a fragmented understanding of the classroom instruction, colored by the evaluator's previous perceptions and experiences with instruction and learning. The teacher often views the process as one of pleasing the evaluator. Development is not acknowledged by either professional. The experience is neither self-generated nor self-renewing. Teachers simply attempt to perform what they perceive as the evaluator's picture of quality teaching performance rather than strive to broaden their understanding of the instructional process.

Additionally, the scheduled observation often is interrupted, denying a fully developed picture of what is really happening in the classroom. Once an observation begins, an administrator may be called out of the classroom to deal with situations that arise and require his or her immediate attention. This results in limited data collection and often does not reflect what is actually happening in the classroom, good or bad. The snapshot of how well a teacher is performing, collected in this manner, cannot depict an accurate portrayal of instructional events.

The teacher development process, on the other hand, requires extended, well-focused time, reflective practice, and collegial conversation. The development process is continual, like a video recording of classroom instruction, rather than episodic, like a snapshot taken at a particular time. Observations of instruction by other educators are at the discretion of the teacher who wants to develop a particular talent. Observations for the purpose of development are frequent and nonjudgmental. The development process details the issues and practices under study and the history of how a teacher investigates instruction and provides a record of developmental progress. Each observation for development isolates an area the teacher designates as one in need of refinement. Then both the developing teacher and the trusted observer engage in collegial reflection and dialogue for the purpose of learning about instructional practice. The capturing and documenting of any instructional act is viewed as an opportunity for collegial investigation. The focus of the development process, unlike evaluation, is not a finished portrait: It is an unfolding landscape of instructional delivery nurtured by the collegial, reflective interactions between teacher and trusted observer.

Teacher learning and collaboration are discouraged. Teachers and administrators rarely are on the same page when it comes to the supervisory process. Administrators view their role as assessors of teacher performance for the purpose of retention, remediation, or removal of teachers who are not performing adequately. Teachers desire constructive feedback to improve their classroom performance and to receive recognition for exemplary instructional methods. Evaluation serves the administrator's mission. It does not promote sharing among professionals, nor does it provide the forum for meaningful, collaborative conversations that lead to informed instructional thinking or reflection upon instructional methodology. The snapshot observation, the product of evaluation, is a piece of paper that denotes the administrator's perception of the observed instructional performance, which is confined to a place and a time and the evaluator's understanding of teaching and learning. It positions the administrator's assessment of the instruction as the principle view of the teacher's performance. The teacher's perception is not considered.

This is most antithetical to professional development. Professional development places teachers at the heart of educational change and requires alternative forms of governance.[14] Meaningful teacher development is teacher driven and encouraged and enriched by collegial interactions. "It is likely that when more teachers have opportunities to collaborate across classrooms, schools, and communities and when they develop their own set of evaluative standards, they will find avenues for broader dissemination, and the value of their work will increase dramatically."[15] Using a process of "collective inquiry," teachers and administrators can share their understandings of teaching and learning in order to improve education for students.[16]

This does not usually happen at most evaluative sessions. Rather, the teacher is judged by the standards of the instrument and the lens of the evaluator, leaving little room for dialogue about instruction. Promising instruction goes no further than the teacher observed and the evaluator's experience of it. Areas of weakness, identified by the evaluator, are left for the teacher to work out alone. In this sense, the evaluation process is a lonely experience for the teacher.

Little or no authentic communication occurs. Little or no authentic communication occurs between teachers and administrators during the current evaluation process. Most teacher evaluation is communicated in one direction, from the administrator to the teacher. In the process, professional development is evaluated with little attention paid to ways teachers evolve expertise in the practice of teaching. Teacher reflection on performance is not a priority in this process of evaluation. It is the evaluator's perceptions that are the emphasis of the communications. The teacher's role is to conform to the vision and expectations of the designated leader of the school—the principal or the principal's appointee. As Andrew Gitlin and Karen Price note, "Teachers are treated as if administrative supervision is necessary to ensure proper behavior."[17]

Such supervisory practice conveys to teachers that administrators and teachers are on opposite sides. They are not a team that inquires. This stunts the growth of the school as a learning organization. Teacher growth relies upon owning development. For evaluation and supervision to conjoin with development, administrators must encourage collective inquiry among members of the school team.[18]

The supervisory/evaluative process is best when it encourages reflective practice and collegiality. Reflecting on instructional performance and sharing issues with each other help teachers emerge as leaders in their professional development. Encouraging teachers to become reflective about instruction in order to understand how their practice is a means for constructing relevant theories about student learning must take hold in the evaluative process if we are to empower teachers to own and value their growth process.

Teaching experience is ignored. Traditional evaluation processes provide little or no consideration for a teacher's level of experience. Regardless of teachers' expertise or years of service, they are all treated the same throughout the evaluation process. Veteran teachers, who are masters of their profession, are treated the same as first-year teachers. There are no opportunities for exemplar teachers to share their insights and talents with others.

By evaluating each teacher in isolation, there are no opportunities for teachers to grow and learn from each other. No latitude is given for the veteran or rookie teacher to observe other professionals, to discuss different pedagogical processes for teaching or motivating students, nor are there occasions for the school to develop shared visions, values, or beliefs for instructional improvement. Evaluation carried out in the traditional mode not only reinforces professional isolation, but also offers no opportunities to share ideas or inquire into best practices, the heart of professional development. As such, it limits the school organization's capacity to develop into a learning organization.

To move toward a more collegial process, supervisors and administrators must be willing to confront the very heart of schooling—the teaching and learning process and the culture in which it occurs. Every educator within the school environment must take responsibility for productive professional development. Most central to the idea of professional development is inquiry among peers. This requires that educators reflect privately and publicly about assumptions, beliefs, and practices of learning and teaching. Educators also must plan together to carry out initiatives, to support each other's experimentation with teaching and learning practices that influence student achievement. Likewise, educators must challenge each other to continually improve, even when the school organization thinks it is the best it can be.

To do this, supervisors and administrators can incorporate principles and strategies, such as collaboration, dialogue, and reflection, to bring about collegiality and a climate receptive to school renewal. A shift toward more collaborative supervisory processes may dispel the sense of isolation inherent in traditional approaches to evaluation. At the very least, it brings about what Wendy Poole describes as a "softening of the hierarchy of supervision."[19] But the willingness to work collaboratively is not enough; structures that support collaboration are also important. To collaborate, dialogue, and reflect together requires authentic relationships among individuals who feel comfortable enough to challenge issues and each other. Collegial dialogue is the bottom line. Without it, nothing changes.

Meaningful dialogue occurs best within trusting relationships. Developing understanding and comfort through active listening, attending to both verbal and nonverbal messages, and appropriate questioning facilitates critical discussions about beliefs, values, and actions and permits adult learning to become an accepted practice. Dialogue also assumes reflection. Reflection is the process of gaining a deeper understanding of the issues, as well as how individuals construct their understandings. One of the most powerful ways that school leaders can affect change is by modeling reflective practice.

No protocol exists through which to communicate. Supervisors and teachers share common interests for dialogue, but not necessarily the same perspectives. What supervisors and administrators choose to discuss and how they share ideas with teachers significantly influence the school's culture. Administrators often underestimate or do not understand the power language and its effect on teacher-supervisor conferences and teacher growth and development. Studies of face-to-face communication have made significant contributions to the body of research on supervision. Yet, these contributions largely have been ignored. An exception is Art Costa and Robert Garmston's popular cognitive coaching model.[20] Even though some researchers estimate that as much as 85% of a supervisor's behavior is talk, many school leaders do not recognize, much less attend to, the effects of their language on others. But language is important. When supervisors see their role as disseminators of information, they tell; when that role shifts to facilitators of understanding, they frame questions and restate their messages.

In a teaching development process, dialogue should suspend opinions so that meaning of ideas emerge. David Bohn refers to this as "participatory consciousness," that is, being able to recognize with awareness that ideas flow between people in order to discover meaning.[21] By practicing participatory consciousness, supervisors, evaluators, and teachers can listen more fully to what each other has to say. They can talk through ideas and issues, realizing each other's assumptions as they learn to appreciate each other's meaning, and find more creative ways of exploring the ideas.

These different linguistic acts asking rather than telling, discourse rather than lecture elicit different responses, sometimes almost too subtle to recognize. For example, in our work with teachers, they are initially impressed by the power of thinking out loud. They make comments such as, "These conferences help me think more clearly," or "I always get such good ideas when we talk." Later, they begin to reflect on the supervisor's language and mention that the way a particular question was asked shifted their thinking. They say they like it when the supervisor respects their thinking by pausing and restating or questioning what he or she heard.

As school practitioners become increasingly aware of their own use of language and more comfortable with linguistic skills, such as active listening and framing questions, they report renewed enthusiasm for talking with colleagues about teaching and learning. Unless supervisors can function as equals with teachers and establish trust and collegiality, neither they nor teachers will grow from their observations and interactions, and the supervisory process will continue to be little more than ritual.[22]

To evolve the tradition mantles of evaluation and supervision to include and sustain genuine professional development of teachers means that educators must abandon outdated models and embrace more collegial conceptions. Charlotte Danielson offers some insight on how to do this.[23] She believes that teacher evaluation is quality assurance for learners and creates a professional learning opportunity for the teacher. Quality assurance emerges when teachers and administrators work together in nonthreatening and nonjudgmental ways to enhance instruction and increase student performance for all learners. Collegial coaching provides such a climate. As administrators and evaluators become more involved in promulgating more collegial environments, learning opportunities are more richly defined for teachers. As teachers grow and develop, it has a reciprocal, powerful effect on student learning.[24]

While a sound evaluation process is a high priority in district policy, budget, and operational practice, it does not take the place of development. In order to warrant teacher development and learning, a codified coaching process and a mentoring program are necessities. By assuring that teachers, both beginning and seasoned, have numerous and ongoing opportunities to engage in collegial conversations and investigations of the teaching/learning process, school districts can more efficiently guarantee quality instruction for learners. As new teachers are mentored into the teaching profession, they learn the structures and operations of the school more efficiently. When mentoring and coaching programs are viewed as priorities, new teachers acclimate to the school culture. All practitioners are exposed to the norms and mores of the school, and occasions for rich dialogues about instruction with new and seasoned teachers are created, reducing the isolation of practice for all.

Organizations, like reflective practitioners, must continually examine what they believe and do in order to grow. The school organization must examine and reexamine the beliefs and actions of everyone within the organization to assure that educational practitioners' beliefs and actions are consistent with desired learning outcomes. Mechanisms that encourage individuals to gently challenge their school's beliefs and actions foster organizational learning. A simple exercise is to encourage each other to ask this question: Why do we do this? Our answers may challenge the very core of our beliefs and practices, but the process fosters growth and consistency between beliefs and actions. As we gingerly nudge each other, school practitioners can begin to transform the school into a collaborative, reflective institution that promotes continual learning and growth for all. When schools operate in this way, they become true learning organizations.[25]

Finally, the confluence of the supervision, evaluation, and development processes involves both teachers and supervisors attaining common understandings about not only the relationships between teaching practices and student learning, but also how we as professional educators work together to create a learning climate for all who participate in our schools. Teacher development requires rigorous investigation into our beliefs and actions as educators and serious study of the teaching/learning process. Teacher development must be collegial and teacher driven in order to provide the necessary autonomy for teachers to determine, shape, and sustain their professional growth. Concomitantly, administrators must understand the distinctions between supervision, evaluation, and development to undertake the initiative of constructing a comprehensive, holistic design for a school that constitutes instructional excellence. In doing so, administrators and supervisors free themselves from an inauthentic, dual, and often conflicting role of assisting teachers in their growth merely by evaluating teachers' instructional delivery.

Notes

1. Andrew Gitlin and Karen Price, "Teacher Empowerment and the Development of Voice," in *Supervision in Transition*, ed. Carl D. Glickman (Washington, D.C.: Association for Supervision and Curriculum Development, 1992), p. 63.

2. Richard DuFour and Robert Eaker, *Professional Learning Communities at Work* (Bloomington, Ind.: National Education Service, 1998).

3. Ann Lieberman and Lynne Miller, "Teacher Development in Professional Practice Schools," in *Professional Practice Schools: Linking Teacher Education and School Reform*, ed. Marsha Levine (New York: Teachers College Press, 1992).

4. Ann Lieberman and Lynne Miller, *Teachers—Transforming Their World and Their Work* (New York: Teachers College Press, 1999), p. 60.

5. Martin Huberman, "Networks That Alter Teaching: Conceptualizations, Exchanges, and Experiments," *Teachers and Teaching: Theory and Practice* 1, no. 2 (1995): 193-211.

6. For a discussion of teaching as a performing art, see Marylou Dantonio, *How Can We Create Thinkers? Questioning Strategies That Work for Teachers* (Bloomington, Ind.: National Education Service, 1990); Marylou Dantonio and Paul Beisenherz, *Learning to Question: Questioning to Learn* (Needham, Mass.: Allyn & Bacon, 2001); Deborah Loewenberg Ball and David K. Cohen, "Developing Practice, Developing Practitioners: Toward a Practice-Based Theory of Professional Education," in *Teaching As the Learning Profession: Handbook of Policy and Practice*, ed. Linda Darling-Hammond and Gary Sykes (San Francisco: Jossey-Bass, 1999), pp. 3-32; and Seymour B. Sarason, *Teaching As a Performing Art* (New York: Teachers College Press, 1999).

7. Charles L. Thompson and John S. Zeuli, "The Frame and the Tapestry: Standards-Based Reform and Professional Development," in *Teaching As the Learning Profession: Handbook of Policy and Practice*, ed. Linda Darling-Hammond and Gary Sykes (San Francisco: Jossey-Bass, 1999), pp. 341-75.

8. Ibid.

9. James Nolan and Pam Francis, "Changing Perspectives in Curriculum and Instruction," in *Supervision in Transition*, ed. Carl D. Glickman (Alexandria, Va.: Association for Supervision and Curriculum Development, 1992).

10. John O'Neil, "Supervision Reappraised," ASCD UPDATE 35, no. 6 (1993): 8.

11. Peter F. Oliva, *Supervision for Today's Schools*, 3rd ed. (New York: Longman, 1989), p. 54.

12. Charlotte Danielson, *Teacher Evaluation to Enhance Professional Development* (Alexandria, Va.: Association for Supervision and Curriculum Development, 2000), p. 3.

13. Jim Nolan, Brent Hawkes, and Pam Francis, "Case Studies: Windows onto Clinical Supervision," *Educational Leadership* 51, no. 2 (1993): 52.

14. Peter P. Grimmett, Olaf P. Rostad, and Blake Ford, "The Transformation of Supervision," in *Supervision in Transition*, ed. Carl D. Glickman (Washington, D.C.: Association for Supervision and Curriculum Development, 1992); Lieberman and Miller, "Teacher Development in Professional Practice

Schools."

15. Marilyn Cochran-Smith and Susan L. Lytle, *Inside/Outside: Teacher Research and Knowledge* (New York: Teachers College Press, l993), p. 19.

16. For a discussion of collective inquiry, see Rick Ross, Bryan Smith, and Charlotte Roberts, "The Team Learning Wheel," in *The Fifth Discipline Fieldbook: Strategies and Tools for Building a Learning Organization*, ed. Peter Senge et al. (New York : Doubleday, 1994), pp. 59-64. See also Nolan and Francis, "Changing Perspectives in Curriculum and Instruction."

17. Gitlin and Price, "Teacher Empowerment and the Development of Voice," 63.

18. Senge et al., *The Fifth Discipline Fieldbook*.

19. Wendy L. Poole, "Removing the Super from Supervision," *Journal of Curriculum and Supervision* 9, no. 3 (1994): 298.

20. *Another Set of Eyes: Conference Skills Part II*, educational consultants Arthur Costa and Robert Garmston, 40 min., Association for Supervision and Curriculum Development, 1989, videocassette. See also, Arthur L. Costa and Robert J. Garmston, *Cognitive Coaching: A Foundation for Renaissance Schools* (Norwood, Mass.: Christopher Gordon Publishers, 1994).

21. David Bohm, *On Dialogue*, ed. Lee Nichol (London: Routledge, 1996), p. 26.

22. Andy Hargreaves and Ruth Dawe, "Paths of Professional Development: Contrived Collegiality, Collaborative Culture, and the Case of Peer Coaching," *Teaching and Teacher Education* 6, no. 3 (1990): 227-41; Noreen B. Garman, "Reflection, the Heart of Clinical Supervision: A Modern Rationale for Professional Practice," *Journal of Curriculum and Supervision* 2, no.1 (1986): 1-24.

23. Danielson, *Teacher Evaluation*, 3.

24. Susan Rosenholtz, *Teachers' Workplace: The Social Organization of Schools* (New York: Teachers College Press, 1989), p. 100.

25. Peter Senge, *The Fifth Discipline: The Art and Practice of the Learning Organization* (New York: Doubleday, 1990); Peter Senge, *Schools That Learn* (New York: Doubleday, 2000).

CHAPTER EIGHT

Administrator's Role

Leadership is not a science or an art, it is a state of consciousness in which we discover the path to our own kingdoms.

— Debashis Chatterjee,
Leading Consciously

The most significant player in establishing a successful collegial coaching program is the principal. The principal is most responsible for creating and sustaining a productive, collegial school climate where teachers can feel comfortable engaging in teacher development and leadership. In the process of instituting a collegial coaching program, principals have to be keenly aware of what the process is, how it best operates, the role they play, and the conditions that must be established in order for teachers to collaborate successfully. This may mean reconsidering the leadership role of the principal.

The notion of principal as school leader is not new. In fact, the current literature promotes the principal as instructional leader as well as leader of reform efforts.[1] Like corporate leaders, principals are responsible for the climate of the organization. Productive and collegial school climates often begin with an examination of the role and definition of leadership. According to Debashis Chatterjee,

> Leaders transform organizations not by imitating other successful organizations but by looking deeply within the traditions of their own organizations. . . . Leaders . . . energize and facilitate the spontaneous flowing of indigenous ideas within the organization. They are indeed the symbolic seeds for inside-out transformation of the organization—metaphors that bring about metamorphosis.[2]

Likewise, effective school leadership is not leadership until it is perceived as shared. It is a relationship among individuals who recognize that leadership is emergent. The principal may be cast in the "official" role; however, to be successful in cultivating a vigorous, healthy school, the principal must be willing to recognize and to encourage emerging leadership among teachers. In this sense, the school is a kingdom of kingdoms.

When leadership is shared, it becomes empowering. Empowerment is especially important when instituting a collegial coaching program. Until the moment this understanding occurs, leadership is merely positioning for power. Thomas Sergiovanni proposes that principals learn to think and act "by purpose and empowerment, 'power to accomplish' rather than 'power over' people and events."[3] An effective leadership style requires flexibility, direction, inclusion, and the ability to facilitate shared values among instructional faculty. By facilitating teacher-inspired learning opportunities, principals have occasion to reestablish themselves as leaders of purpose and empowerment.

Teachers traditionally have had little control over policy; therefore, it is the principal who is responsible for creating and supporting the appropriate environment for collegial coaching to be a successful schoolwide initiative. Teachers' perceptions of their principal as an instructional leader are powerful determinants of teachers' satisfaction with their own professional roles. When teachers view their principal as a collaborative leader who exhibits behaviors and beliefs aligned with the principles of coaching, teachers are more likely to engage the collegial coaching process, using it as a vehicle for learning about teaching.[4] When instituting a collegial coaching program for teacher development, two factors emerge as especially important: (1) how principals encourage teacher empowerment and (2) the type and extent of administrative support. A principal's attitudes and beliefs about these factors will help to determine teacher success in carrying out a collegial coaching process. These issues are addressed as they relate to fostering a spirit of camaraderie among education professionals within the school context.

The first factor, empowering teachers, is pivotal to establishing a collegial norm for experimentation and inquiry into instructional practices. The respect, trust, and confidence principals have for teachers' abilities to influence their own development are essential to building a strong collegial school culture that fosters teacher talent development. This perspective, evidenced not only through what is said but also through what is done, needs to be communicated convincingly and shared by teachers and administrators in the school. Principals' convictions about teacher professional development are played out in their commitment to providing appropriate workplace conditions.

The second factor, a supportive administration, serves to strengthen communication and interdependence among teachers and other school personnel and builds the foundation for linking instructional practices with student achievement. Samuel Krug's study of school leaders reveals that a principal's understanding of the importance of the school's mission and instructional climate, active nurturing of teacher professional development, and linking student evaluation data to curriculum planning and instructional design are significant factors in student achievement.[5]

How teachers feel about their workplace influences the success they have in their own professional development and the effect they have on student learning. The following six dimensions reflect the psychological climate of a workplace:

• Supportive management the extent to which people feel supported by their manager;

- Claritythe degree of clarity about what is expected of an individual;
- Contribution the feeling that one's contribution is worthwhile;
- Recognition the feeling that one's contribution is recognized and appreciated;
- Self-expression feeling free to question the way things are done; and
- Challenge the feeling that one's work is challenging.[6]

Each of these dimensions is an indicator of teachers' perceived safety to experiment with instruction, to study themselves as educators, and to engage in meaningful instructional leadership. For principals to play a critical role in creating and sustaining a productive, collegial school climate where teachers feel comfortable engaging in teacher development and leadership, they too must participate in learning about teaching with their instructional school team.

Susan Rosenholtz's study of teachers' workplaces affirms that principals who provide and participate in opportunities for teachers to share in decision making on instructional issues and who facilitate teachers coming together to discuss school goals provide the foundation for collective inquiry into educational issues.[7] Rosenholtz identifies three conditions affecting professional development and their implications for teachers and student learning:

> First, teachers' empowerment—their task autonomy and discretion—gives them the sense that student growth and development result directly from their own instructional efforts. Second, teachers' learning opportunities offer them a sense of ongoing challenge and continuous growth that makes greater mastery and control of their environment possible. Third, teachers' psychic rewards ensure their continuous contributions to the school.[8]

Rosenholtz cautions that to neglect these workplace conditions "carries negative and far-reaching consequences for teachers. They become disaffected and alienated from their work, they absent themselves frequently, or they desire to leave the workplace altogether. Teachers' lack of motivation and commitment, as manifested in a lack of future planning and in complacency with the present, is visited on students through their diminished opportunity to learn basic skills."[9] Rosenholtz concludes that there is a correlation between student achievement and schools where principals exhibit strong beliefs and policies about teacher autonomy and collegiality. Peter Grimmett and his colleagues observe that through development of a collegial culture, "teachers experience a heightened sense of teaching efficacy and professional empowerment. They become purposeful and enterprising in their actions. . . . Developing instructional practice becomes an important professional choice that motivates such teachers to become visionary about what can happen in teaching and learning. In short, they take care of their professional lives and engage in perpetual learning about their craft."[10]

Principals can effect a prosperous school culture for emerging teacher learning and leadership by supporting the concept of collaborative study groups. Collaborative study groups provide school practitioners opportunities to focus on learning about teaching, develop a common value system, and cultivate a collegial environment for experimentation with instruction. Richard DuFour and Robert Eaker note, "Collaborative team learning focuses on organizational renewal and a willingness to work together in a continuous improvement process."[11] To create such learning opportunities for teachers requires that principals support structures for encouraging the development of shared goals and common purposes; establishing time and space for professional interactions that focus on studying and experimenting with instructional practices; and developing and implementing operational structures for teacher collaboration to enhance teachers' reflection, technical competence, and confidence about instruction.

Establishing and nurturing teacher learning opportunities and collaborative study groups returns to the teaching profession the dignity, decency, and decorum necessary for teacher growth and development. The payoff is the great influence the collegial school culture has on student achievement.[12] Quite simply, the role of the principal is most critical in establishing a workplace conducive to teacher learning. Collegial coaching can provide the structure for professional learning and instructional leadership to sprout and bloom. However, it is the principal who must consciously decide that professional collegiality, collaboration, and experimentation with teaching and learning are important enough to empower teachers to lead themselves to inquire into the teaching self. The principal can cultivate a school climate that nurtures teacher growth and emerging leadership, or the principal can neglect the soil so that little will grow. The choice is the principal's to make.

Notes

1. Wilma F. Smith, "Leadership for Educational Renewal," *Phi Delta Kappan* 80, no. 8 (1999): 602-05.

2. Debashis Chatterjee, *Leading Consciously: A Pilgrimage Toward Self-Mastery* (Boston: Butterworth-Heinemann, 1998), pp. 125-26.

3. Thomas Sergiovanni, "The Theoretical Basis for Cultural Leadership," in *Leadership: Examining the Elusive*, ed. Linda Sheive and Marian B. Schoenheit, (Alexandria, Va.: Association for Supervision and Curriculum Development, 1987), p.122.

4. Wilma F. Smith and Richard L. Andrews, *Instructional Leadership: How Principals Make a Difference* (Alexandria, Va.: Association for Supervision and Curriculum Development, 1989).

5. Samuel E. Krug, "Leadership Craft and the Crafting of School Leaders," *Phi Delta Kappan* 75, no. 3 (1993): 240-44.

6. Doc Lew Childre and Bruce Cryer, *From Chaos to Coherence: Advancing Emotional and Organizational Intelligence Through Inner Quality Management* (Boston: Butterworth-Heinemann, 1999), p. 163.

7. Susan J. Rosenholtz, *Teachers' Workplace: The Social Organization of Schools* (New York: Longman, 1989).

8. Ibid., p. 7.

9. Ibid.

10. Peter P. Grimmett, Olaf P. Rostad, and Blake Ford, "The Transformation of Supervision," in *Supervision in Transition*, ed. Carl D. Glickman (Alexandria, Va.: Association for Supervision and Curriculum Development, 1992), p. 186.

11. Richard DuFour and Robert Eaker, *Professional Learning Communities at Work: Best Practices for Enhancing Student Achievement* (Bloomington, Ind.: National Educational Service, 1988; Alexandria, Va.: Association for Supervision and Curriculum Development, 1998), p. 27; Smith and Andrews, *Instructional Leadership*; and Smith, "Leadership for Educational Renewal."

12. Catherine A. Lugg and William L. Boyd, "Leadership for Collaboration: Reducing Risk and Fostering Resilience," *Phi Delta Kappan* 75, no. 3 (1993): 253-58; Martin L. Maehr and Stephanie A. Parker, "A Tale of Two Schools—and the Primary Task of Leadership," *Phi Delta Kappan* 75, no. 3 (1993): 233-39; and Rosenholtz, *Teachers' Workplace*.

Part Two
Practice

CHAPTER NINE

Instituting Coaching in
A Collegial School Environment

The seeds of development will not grow if they are cast on stony ground.
— Andy Hargreaves and Michael Fullan,
Understanding Teacher Development

Collegial coaching is predicated on a set of conditions identified through research. These define the professional learning environment, attitudes, and values necessary for implementing successful programs in teacher development and leadership. Ann Lieberman and Lynne Miller have identified the following five conditions for a school culture that supports teachers' inquiry into practice:

- norms of colleagueship, openness, and trust;
- opportunities and time for disciplined inquiry;
- teacher learning of content in context;
- reconstruction of leadership roles; and
- networks, collaborations, and coalitions.[1]

Each of these is essential in establishing a successful collegial coaching program. The conditions underscore the care that must be paid to the environment in which teachers work. Ignore just one and any other efforts to build an effective collegial coaching program will be negated.

When teachers engage in the study of instructional practice to inform their instructional delivery, they are carrying out the actions of teacher educators. Teacher educators must be adept observers of teaching, curious about practice, think in many ways about students, instructional deliveries, and how to best communicate their content to learners.[2] Teacher educators are students of teaching practice. As classroom teachers engage in the role of teacher educator, they must be cognizant of how teachers learn about teaching, especially if they engage in using the collegial coaching process to carry out their studies in teaching.

Collegial coaching is based on five premises, each of which is discussed below.

Premise One

No one can force another person to change his or her teaching behavior. It is up to the individual teacher to change. Every teacher must recognize her or his own teaching behaviors that need to be developed, and she or he must want to change inappropriate or ineffective practices. In the collegial coaching process, the coach acts as a facilitator, counselor, and interviewer. The coach does not have the power to change a particular teaching practice: That choice lies with the teacher.

The coach participates in the process by carefully questioning the teacher's actions and assumptions in an effort to assist the teacher in reflecting on problems that occur during classroom instruction. The coach trusts and respects the teacher's commitment and ability to solve such problematic situations. In this supportive climate, the teacher is encouraged to take the necessary steps to develop her or his teaching talents.

Premise Two

Instructional improvement relies on objective and descriptive reporting of teaching behaviors. Teachers are developed, not born, and teaching can be analyzed. The coach must be seen not only as supportive of the teacher's efforts, but also as adept at observing classroom practices.

The aptitude of the coach's observational skills is revealed as the coach guides the teacher through deliberations and analyses of her or his classroom performance. The coach must be able to analyze teaching performance in the same manner that a football coach analyzes plays and engages the athlete in fine tuning the execution of particular skills or techniques. At times, it may be necessary for the coach to model a technique for the teacher. When the coach serves as a model, the teacher can form a mental picture that will influence his or her classroom performance. The coach needs to be well acquainted with the skill or methodology in a variety of teaching contexts in order to assist teachers in solving problems they may encounter.

Premise Three

Coaching is an ongoing, reflective, decision-making process. Instructional improvement is never-ending. In coaching, the study of teaching must be integrated into the school schedule and conducted throughout the school year, continuing each year of service in a teacher's career. Research has shown that there is an inverse relationship between the mean number of years of teaching experience and teaching effectiveness.[3] Simply because we introduce teachers to new innovations and techniques does not guarantee that they will want to use them or will use them effectively in the classroom. Whether or not a teacher will develop a refined teaching repertoire appears to depend on how she or he thinks about learning to teach. Susan Rosenholtz found that in schools where teachers share the idea that learning to teach is a life-long, continual process that matures as one continues to teach, teachers value their learning opportunities.[4]

The process of professional growth requires that teachers have opportunities to discover their individual needs, strengths, and ways of contributing to the development of their talents. Talent development in the performing arts blends practice and critique prior to performance to attain a degree of competence in delivery. Practice and critique are separated from the performance.

Unfortunately, teachers always have an audience. This makes it difficult to focus on technique development alone. Collegial coaching provides opportunities for a teacher to concentrate on working with students while the coach attends to collecting information about teaching skills and techniques.

Like other performing artists who grow, change, and mature throughout their careers, teachers must constantly engage in the study of their practice. By studying teaching, experimenting with content and methods, and practicing delivery, teachers become both consumers of knowledge and producers of practical theories. Teachers begin to use practices specific to the context of their own classrooms, and they have opportunities to conduct inquiry into the knowledge base for learning and teaching that is grounded in practice.[5]

Premise Four

Collaboration among educators in a school community is a process of attraction. "The process and success of teacher development depends very much on the context in which it takes place."[6] A collegial, trusting, nurturing school culture is both the foundation and the goal of a productive learning environment for teachers and students. However, teachers must choose to use collegial coaching as a process for talent development. Collaboration cannot be mandated. Simply having the opportunity to participate in the collegial development process does not guarantee that teachers will be willing to participate. A teacher's choice not to participate must be respected.

Furthermore, the leadership that emerges when teachers work with each other is the result of individuals' desires to contribute to the professional development of others. This role should not be appointed by the administration. Nor should teachers deemed expert by school administrators or outside authorities be required to provide leadership. Some expert teachers want only to teach children, not teachers. Likewise, some expert teachers could never become expert at coaching because they have not and cannot analyze what makes them effective in teaching. They are good teachers, not effective teachers of teachers. Teachers' sponsorships of one another are not rewards for being good at teaching. Teacher leadership is an evolutionary process. Teachers grow into teachers of teachers.

This may require that building administrators give up some preconceived notions about how teachers should participate in school development programs. Teachers will opt to coach or opt not to coach. They cannot be forced, bribed, enticed, or demeaned into engaging in collegial development. Teachers must see the development process as something that enriches their teaching efforts and reduces the stress of classroom performance. Similarly, teachers must feel that they have the support and trust of the school administration to experiment with development processes without being evaluated. As teachers select a collegial development process, they must be permitted to choose who coaches them and whom they coach.

In order for teachers to feel comfortable collaborating, the predominant norm of teacher isolation must be challenged. It is well documented that teachers work in isolated arenas, either self-imposed or traditional. Unlocking the norm of isolation is the key to fostering a collegial school culture. The norm of isolation, however, is a double-edged sword.

On the one hand, isolation protects the teacher from criticism. On the other hand, classroom solitude prevents teachers from working with each other to develop teaching talents and shared instructional practices. In order for teachers to engage in personal, professional development, pervasive isolation must be diminished and replaced by a community of inquiring educators. The manner in which this is done, however, is extremely important. Teachers must feel that it is safe to join together in the pursuit of effective teaching development. They cannot be mandated to leave what they see as a safe haven.

The success of a collegial coaching program relies on a school culture that encourages experimentation and inquiry into the study of teaching. In examining studies of staff development, Judith Little determined that norms of colleagueship and experimentation are essential for the success of new programs.[7] In collegial coaching, the responsibility and authority for professional growth rest with teachers. However, the emergence of a productive, collegial school environment is the responsibility of all educators within the school community.

Again, the school climate and the tone for implementing collegial coaching, which are established by the administration, are crucial to the outcomes of the process. Without appropriate attention from administrators for the learning climate, the effects on instructional practice and student learning will be nominal. It must be remembered at all times that "teacher development is not only the renewal of teaching, but also the renewal of schools. Teacher development is, in effect, culture building."[8]

Premise Five

Time for teacher collaboration must be important enough to be included in the school schedule. Collegial coaching is a time-intensive professional development activity. In order to engage in this productive inquiry of teaching, teachers need time and space to confer, observe, reflect, and frame and solve instructional problems. As Harold Stevenson observes, "Effective teaching requires time for preparation and knowledge of what is to be taught and how to teach it. Teachers need the time, as well as the training and freedom from other responsibilities, to help their students master the subject matter. They need opportunities to observe and discuss excellent teaching and to share their knowledge with other teachers."[9]

Time is a scarce commodity in the school day. Yet, teacher professional development is integrally linked with student achievement. Therefore, it must be important enough to schedule in a school's daily and weekly events. Administrators must think creatively about ways of freeing time so that teachers may collaborate and contribute to the development of each others' professional teaching talents.

There are many ways to do this. Administrators can take over teachers' classes so that teachers can observe one another. This has several benefits. It demonstrates to teachers that administrators are willing to provide support for teacher development efforts. Second, it may illustrate to teachers that administrators have not lost their teaching touch. Concurrently, it builds rapport between administrators and teachers.

Another means of freeing time is to hire a floating substitute. The substitute teacher can move from classroom to classroom, allowing different teachers time to confer and observe each other. If substitutes are unavailable, trusted parents can be enlisted to release teachers part of the day. This has the potential to help parents understand the concept and benefits of teacher talent development. The community is more likely to support something they have had a hand in creating. When parents participate in the effort to release teachers to collaborate and observe teaching practices, they have a first-hand look at the powerful impact collegial development can have on student learning.

Instituting a successful collegial coaching program takes concerted effort from all educators. Administrators must be clearly aware of what the process is, how it operates, what their role is, and what conditions must be attended to in order for teachers to participate successfully in collegial coaching. Often this means viewing leadership as shared by administrators and teachers. Teachers are viewed as active agents in promoting and engaging in instructional leadership. Also, teachers need the trust and commitment of their administration in finding solutions to barriers that can impede their progress and growth. Without a supportive administration that facilitates opportunities for teachers to share ideas and work together, teachers most likely will not engage in coaching or other leadership efforts.

Fostering the Collegial Culture

Knowing the attributes of a collegial culture and understanding teacher development from a performing arts perspective are quite different from applying these concepts in practice. The importance of sharing a vision about teacher development from a performing arts perspective cannot be underestimated. Successful implementation of collegial coaching requires that administrators and teachers alike perceive teaching as a performing art.

To develop this shared vision, educators in the school community must engage in a common set of experiences that change traditional images and mind sets about teacher development. The following activity is one way of helping teachers and administrators accomplish this task. It is an inductive process that requires educators to rethink the role of the teacher and how teaching talent is developed.

Imaging Activity

This is a group activity that should be conducted by a teacher facilitator who is familiar with the collegial coaching process. During the imaging activity, the teacher should record all responses on a large sheet of paper, such as newsprint, or a blackboard. To assure that participants have an opportunity to respond and understand each others' ideas, the teacher facilitator needs to ask clarifying questions, for example, What do you mean by "ability to bring a character to life?" In order to increase participation, redirecting questions need to be asked, such as, Who else thinks performing artists study their craft? Why do you think that? What other characteristics can you think of that are true of performing artists?[10]

By answering these kinds of questions, participants should be able to develop an understanding and appreciation of the developmental process experienced by performing artists in other fields. After exploring the attributes of performing artists, participants should be able to apply these qualities to themselves as teachers. In concluding the activity, the facilitator should make sure that teachers have insights about themselves as performing artists. Participants should begin to share ideas about how they can use growth processes similar to artists in order to develop teaching talents.

Name some people you admire in other performing arts, for example, actors, musicians, figure skaters, gymnasts, dancers? (Make a list.)

What do you admire about them? (Make a list and explore responses.)

In what ways do they develop their talents? (Make a list and explore responses.)

In what ways are teachers like performing artists? (Explore responses.)

Keeping in mind the image of teachers as performing artists, how might teachers' instructional talents be developed? (Make a list and explore responses.)

In what ways must the development of teachers change for it to be more like the development of performing artists? (Make a list and explore responses.)

In what ways can teachers participate in the professional growth of other teachers? (Make a list and distribute widely.)

What conditions are necessary for teachers to take an active role in assisting teacher growth, development, and leadership opportunities? (Make a list and distribute widely.)

Notes

1. Ann Lieberman and Lynne Miller, "Teacher Development in Professional Practice Schools," in *Professional Practice Schools: Linking Teacher Education and School Reform*, ed. Marsha Levine (New York: Teachers College Press, 1992), p. 7.

2. Deborah Loewenberg Ball and David K. Cohen, "Developing Practice, Developing Practitioners: Toward a Practice-Based Theory of Professional Education," in *Teaching As the Learning Profession: Handbook of Policy and Practice*, ed. Linda Darling-Hammond and Gary Sykes (San Francisco: Jossey-Bass, 1999).

3. Thomas L. Good and Jere E. Brophy, *Looking in Classrooms*, 4th ed. (New York: Harper and Row, l987); Martin T. Katzman, *The Political Economy of Urban Schools* (Cambridge, Mass.: Harvard University Press, l971).

4. Susan J. Rosenholtz, *Teachers' Workplace: The Social Organization of Schools* (New York: Longman, 1989).

5. Marilyn Cochran-Smith and Susan L. Lytle, *Inside/Outside: Teacher Research and Knowledge* (New York: Teachers College Press, 1993); Rosenholtz, *Teachers' Workplace*.

6. Andy Hargreaves and Michael G. Fullan, *Understanding Teacher Development* (New York: Teachers College Press, l992), p. 13.

7. Judith W. Little, "Norms of Collegiality and Experimentation: Workplace Conditions of School Success," *American Educational Research Journal* 19, no. 3 (1982): 325-40, and Judith W. Little, "Seductive Images and Organizational Realities in Professional Development," in *Rethinking School Improvement: Research, Craft, and Concept*, ed. Ann Lieberman (New York: Teachers College Press, l986), pp. 26-34.

8. Lieberman and Miller, "Teacher Development in Professional Practice Schools," p. 106.

9. Harold W. Stevenson, "Why Asian Students Still Outdistance Americans," *Educational Leadership* 50, no. 5, (l993): 65.

10. Marylou Dantonio, *How Can We Create Thinkers? Questioning Strategies that Work for Teachers* (Bloomington, Ind.: National Educational Service, 1990).

CHAPTER TEN

Planning Conference

The planning conference is a focused, communal journey into pedagogical thinking with a trusted colleague. Of the two conferences in the cycle, it is the most important one. Here the coaching partners prepare for delivery by thinking through the lesson as the teacher envisions it unfolding in the classroom. Once teachers become comfortable with the planning conference process, it usually requires 20 or 30 minutes of their time. (It should be noted that the planning conference is not the same as a prelesson conference in the clinical supervision model. In clinical supervision, the prelesson conference is a brief encounter between the observing supervisor or administrator and the teacher designed to provide the observer with information about the teacher's lesson objectives and format for the purpose of evaluation.) The planning conference in collegial coaching is an opportunity for teachers to obtain a frame of reference about the intended classroom instruction.

The coach uses the Planning Conference Question Guide (see page 66) to steer the partners through the conference. When asking questions, the coach needs to attend carefully to the teacher's responses and clarify any that are vague. The order and sequence of the questions provide a framework for uncovering the teacher's ideas about instruction. Based on the teacher's responses, the coach may need to adjust the phrasing and sequence of the questions.

As the coaching partners work together to prepare the teacher for instructional delivery, they build trust and confidence in each other, forming a collegial bond. Additionally, the planning conference offers the coaching partners an opportunity to frame knowledge about teaching and learning. The teacher's role is to determine what is to occur in the classroom, and the coach's role is to understand the teacher's reasoning.

This dual aim—forming a collegial bond and framing knowledge—often creates tension as the coaching partners balance climate building with instructional analysis. This tension can be alleviated by the coach's approach to the conference. Effective coaching teachers are indirect and empathize with other teachers through body language. The coach's major objective is to help the teacher feel comfortable while investigating the fine details of the lesson.

As the planning conference unfolds, the coaching partners run through a dress rehearsal of the teacher's lesson plan. The rehearsal engages the partners in "professional talk" as they envision the events that will occur in the classroom.[1] Here the goal is for the teacher and coach to develop frames of knowing about instruction by thinking through how a specific lesson will be enacted with children. Frames of knowing are based on emerging knowledge about teaching, originating in classroom teaching experiences.[2]

During this conference, the coaching partners have an opportunity to identify the content, the sequence of activities, the behaviors of students, and the relationships between teaching practices and learner outcomes; they can also anticipate potential problems. The coach carefully questions the teacher's assumptions about various instructional practices and the anticipated effects these practices will have on students' learning. The coaching partners use this time to investigate the academic, social, and personal implications of instruction inherent in the teacher's beliefs.

In other words, the coaching partners think about how they think about teaching. This deliberation contributes to how teachers perform in the classroom.[3] Barry Beyer observes, "Thinking becomes more effective and efficient when we think about how we are thinking as we think."[4] As discussions continue, teacher and coach form a common mindset or shared way of thinking about the lesson and the intended results. This mindset has been referred to previously as "peer vision."

Teachers plan lessons in different ways.[5] Some teachers create very detailed pictures of the instructional process, paying great attention to what they are going to do; others map out general activities. They often think of students and the content they want to teach when planning. Some teachers are very sketchy in their planning, writing down only what administrators want to see. Some let their intuitions work for them, envisioning activities as they drive home from school or relax at home. No matter how planning is articulated—written or spoken—preparation is essential to achieve learning outcomes with children as well as to enhance and refine teaching talents. Being prepared for the events of instruction takes shape only when teachers put time and energy into visualizing themselves delivering the lesson.

As teachers coach novice and experienced teachers, they must be cognizant of how experience affects the development of lesson plans. It is well documented that novice teachers have difficulty planning.[6] Experienced teachers often rely on their prior teaching experiences and do not make explicit, written lesson plans.[7] Additionally, the coach must be flexible in assisting teachers in refining lesson plans. It is not the coach's job to plan a teacher's lesson or to change the teacher's plan. The coach acts as a sounding board for the teacher to share plans, instructional practices, and theories about instruction. The coach assists the teacher in deliberating on the practices prior to the lesson's implementation so that the teacher may refine them.

Since prior experience contributes to building practical theories about instruction, novice teachers will not have the same coaching needs as experienced teachers. Novice teachers typically have not examined their practices to ascertain an understanding of the nature of learners and the conditions necessary for effective instructional delivery. Beginning teachers have not had sufficient experience to generate tacit relationships between teaching and learning. As for those who have been teaching for some time but exhibit novice characteristics, they need to be guided in reflecting on their teaching experience in order to identify explicitly their assumptions about teaching and learning.

When the coach forms a partnership with an experienced teacher who has attained some degree of expertise in teaching, the coaching partners can have an informative exchange of ideas, concepts, and principles, relating them to the lesson being planned and previous instructional experiences. Through their conversations, the coaching partners develop more in-depth ways of thinking about teaching and learning. The dialogue that occurs throughout the planning conference should assist teachers in better applying instructional techniques, strategies, or skills contextually.

The success of the planning conference rests on the commitment of teachers to investigate instructional processes as they pertain to student learning. There are four specific topics that must be covered during the planning conference. Although these appear linear, they are recursive. The four topics are:

- clarification of lesson goals and objectives;
- decisions about instructional strategies;
- focus of the observation; and
- needs of the teacher and affirmations for accomplishment.

Clarification of Lesson Goals and Objectives

The intent, expected problems, and outcomes of instruction and the anticipated on- and off-task student behaviors are specified by identifying and clarifying goals and objectives. For the coaching partners, establishing a clear mental picture of the intent and direction of the lesson is extremely important. This picture will guide the teacher in lesson delivery, and most likely it will be used to develop the observation instrument used during the teaching performance.

In discussing the lesson's intent, the coaching partners explore the cognitive, social, and personal dimensions of the lesson. What content is important? How will students interact during the lesson? What emotions does the teacher want the students to experience? How will the classroom be arranged for the learning activities? They consider how the lesson will affect students. For example, if the teacher says that the purpose of a lesson on twentieth century English literature is for students to discuss and know the attributes of the character Jane Eyre, then the coaching partners need to explore what is meant by "discuss," "know," and "attribute."

Establishing a clear picture of the purpose of the lesson helps illuminate activities, teaching actions, and student behaviors. While it can be argued that teachers do this when they develop lesson plans, the act of explaining something aloud to someone else can draw out fine details. Also, by engaging in professional talk with a trusted colleague, the opportunity arises for analyzing the teacher's embedded assumptions about instruction. The coaching partners have occasion to discuss whether or not the teacher's instructional practices match these assumptions.

To illustrate, an English teacher says the goal of teaching literature is for students to relate the theme or themes within a given work to their lives. In planning a lesson, the teacher develops a brief introductory lecture about a work of literature that includes a discussion of events relevant to students. Following this introduction, the teacher intends to ask students to answer questions related to characterization, plot, and themes by recalling events of the story. As a final strategy, the teacher intends to ask the students to write their own stories using themes derived from the work.

While the lesson's introduction is intended to illustrate the practicality of the themes in the particular work, using only recall questions during the main lesson may not provide students themselves with opportunities to think about how the themes relate to events in their lives. By closing the lesson with a writing assignment to create a personal story using the literature's themes, students may or may not be able to construct realistic narratives, since, during the instruction, the teacher focused on recalling the events of the story.

During the planning conference, the coach could question the teacher concerning the value of recalling the characters, plot, and theme as these relate to students' real-world, practical experiences. The teacher can rethink how she or he might phrase questions so that there is a direct relationship between events in the story and events in students' lives. Also, the coaching partners can role play students behaviors during the lesson to predict if the questions elicit the kinds of responses that will achieve the teacher's goal. Through prudent questioning, the coach can probe the teacher's ideas about how such instructional practices will bring about the desired ends. This probing enables the teacher to become more sensitive to the delicate balance that exists between teaching practices and learning activities for students.

Questions that stimulate this awakening must be open and allow the teacher to create a problem focus for the intended instruction, that is, what the teacher wants to find out about students' understanding of the content.[8] Determining the issues to be explored and resolved as the teacher orchestrates learning opportunities requires that the coach ask questions that ferret out answers about the teacher's intentions, ideas about students, and tacit assumptions about the teaching/learning process.

To develop a common understanding of language used by the teacher, the coach should clarify terms and phrases after the teacher has answered each question. Specific language to be clarified might include words such as "learn," "discuss," "know," and "bring about an understanding." Once the teacher's purpose and rationale for the lesson are understood by both persons, the coach can assist the teacher in exploring potential problems that could surface while conducting the lesson. The coach can ask probing questions that help the teacher articulate her or his practical theories about instruction, for example, What problems do you anticipate happening during the lesson?

How will you know when things are not going well? How will you deal with these situations? Asking about prior events or experiences that led to such insights provides an opportunity for the teacher to build on her or his knowledge base by tying it to the lesson at hand.

A third consideration in clarifying the lesson's intent is related to student outcomes. The coach must assist the teacher in verbalizing the gains to be made by students by asking questions that help teachers connect intended outcomes to student actions. These include, What will students learn from the activities of the lesson? What do you expect in terms of student outcomes? What specifically will you be looking for in terms of student behaviors if you are successful in achieving the goals and objectives of the lesson? What will students be doing in each activity? What will they look like as they do it? What makes you think that the student behaviors you envision are appropriate for the goals and objectives of your lesson? How will your behaviors influence the student outcomes?

Answers to these questions help establish the framework for lesson execution. As the coaching partners attend to the big picture and the details for delivering the instruction, the events of the lesson are illuminated. The teacher's answers to the questions assist the coach in comprehending how the teacher thinks about the lesson and the teacher's reasons for engaging in the use of specific practices. Thus, the coach has a preview of what is to come and is better prepared to observe the lesson using the teacher's frame of reference.

Decisions about Instructional Strategies

During collegial coaching—especially during the planning conference—the teacher is center stage. It is important that both teacher and coach be able to envision instructional strategies as they are supposed to unfold with students, but such discussions should focus on what the teacher will be doing to achieve the lesson's goals and objectives. All actions on the part of the teacher will in some way affect the learning outcomes for students. Therefore, it is important that the coaching partners attend to the interactive nature of the relationship between teacher practices and student behaviors. At the same time, the coach and teacher must also realize that improvisation will occur during the lesson's implementation.[9] Not only does the coach assist in gaining a perspective on what the teacher plans to do and how the instruction will affect learners, but also the coach plants the seeds for improvising, if needed, during delivery.

The instructional strategies are discussed first in general and then in sequence to create a cognitive map that links one activity to the next with appropriate transitions. As was the case in discussing the lesson's purpose, the coach inquires into reasons for using particular strategies to assist the teacher in understanding implications of both theory and practice. To help the teacher understand the relationship between the planned strategies and student learning, the coach should ask introspective questions aimed at exploring student responses, such as, What makes these strategies appropriate for this lesson? What are you expecting students to do in each of the activities guided by your strategies? How will you assure that students are behaving in ways that are appropriate for achieving the learning outcomes?

A teacher's answers help isolate each instructional activity of the lesson, thereby enabling the teacher to reflect on the appropriateness of each strategy for the intended learning outcomes. Every question should be framed in a manner that helps the teacher see herself or himself engaged in the strategy and simultaneously uncovers any questions the teacher may have about the lesson or practices. As the discussion evolves, often the focus for observation begins to surface. The coach then can explore with the teacher a more specific focus. Both plan how best to provide descriptive, constructive feedback to the teacher about the instructional events to take place during the lesson.

Focus of the Observation

It is important for the coaching partners to determine the observation focus. The impetus for the observation originates with the teacher. During planning conference discussions, problematic aspects of the lesson will become apparent, and the teacher will feel the need to have another perspective on the instructional activity. Whatever is to be observed must be specific. The exact focus should be agreed upon by both teacher and coach. The coach should observe only one behavior, practice, or skill at a time.

For example, the coach can observe a teacher's use of questions or record the number of times that students are not on task or count the number of times the teacher relocates in the room. The purpose for the observation is not to evaluate the effects of the instruction; it is to help the teacher attend to a skill, behavior, or an approach to instruction. The coach provides objective information that the teacher can use to make informed decisions about future teaching actions.

Before observing, the coaching partners must also decide how the focus will be observed. They must choose a method of recording the observation that is both efficient and comfortable for the coach. It may be a chart; it may be a video recording; it may be a floor plan of the classroom. Whatever the form, it must graphically depict teacher actions or student behaviors. It could produce a count of the number of questions a teacher asks, for example, or the number of times a teacher uses indiscriminate praise. It could map the direction of dialogue exchanges between the teacher and students in the classroom. Rarely is the observation tool a standardized form. Regardless of the means of recording, it must concretely represent the identified focus.

Questions that can assist the coaching partners in developing the observation instrument include, What is it that you think needs to be observed? How can we best represent it? In what way will this representation tell us what we are looking for? What is your expectation of how I should communicate feedback to you? The important thing for the coaching partners to remember in designing the observation instrument is that it must be functional in communicating specific, observable, non-evaluative information about the specific focus for observation determined by the teacher. It never is an evaluation form.

Needs of the Teacher and Affirmations for Accomplishments

The culminating phase of the planning conference is assuring that the observation focus is clearly understood and that all the teacher's concerns about the lesson have been addressed. Coach and teacher restate exactly what is to be focused on and why as well as determine what each will do to contribute to the effectiveness of the lesson. At this point, the teacher must communicate her or his expectations of the coach. If the teacher feels threatened or uncomfortable about conducting parts of the lesson, for example, she or he may ask the coach to assist by conducting a specific portion of the lesson while the teacher observes the coach and records information. Additionally, equipment needs are discussed, with the coach acting as a resource. Roles are clarified and responsibilities are confirmed.

Questions the coach can use to guide this discussion include, What anxieties are you experiencing? How can I help you feel more comfortable? To reaffirm the observation focus the coach might ask the teacher to restate what she or he wants the coach to look for, what she or he wants the coach to do during the lesson, and how the coach can best communicate to the teacher following the lesson. The coach might also reconfirm any assistance or resources needed for the lesson. Teachers' answers will help solidify roles and relationships and establish the foundation for a successful observation experience, while confirming the trust necessary to reinforce the collegial relationship.

The planning conference is a journey into professional, collegial dialogue about teaching and the development of teaching talent. For the teacher, it is a venture in discovering and understanding the intricacies of teaching practices and the relationship of these to student learning. It spotlights the classroom and the anticipated learning events. It provides a safe haven for rehearsing lessons and reflecting on the lesson's potential effects. For the coach, it provides an opportunity to learn about another teacher's beliefs, assumptions, strategies, and experiences. The planning conference is fertile ground for nurturing a collegial relationship. As the coaching partners grow in their frames of knowing about instruction and how instructional development occurs, they contribute to enhancing the teaching talent of their profession.

Planning Conference Question Guide

Clarification of Lesson Goals and Objectives

What is the intent of the lesson?

What is meant by specific words in your statement of the lesson's purpose?

What assumptions are you making about the learners?

What problems are you anticipating?

How will you know when lesson plans are going well?

How will you know when lesson plans are not going well?

What events or actions will lead you to these conclusions?

How will you adjust your lesson plan if students are not responding as you expected?

What will students learn from the activities of the lesson?

What do you anticipate that students will be doing during this particular activity?

What will their overall expressions be as they do it?

How do your behaviors influence the students' behaviors?

How will your behaviors be influenced by students?

How will you determine if you are successful in achieving the goals and objectives of the lesson?

What behaviors are you looking for in students if they achieve the goals and objectives?

What makes you think that the student behaviors envisioned are appropriate for the goals and objectives?

Decisions about Instructional Strategies

What strategies will you be using?

What makes them appropriate for this lesson?

What are you expecting students to do in each of the activities guided by your strategies?

How will you assure that students are behaving in ways appropriate for achieving the learning outcomes?

In what order will you conduct the strategies?

Why this order?

Focus of the Observation

What is it that needs to be observed?

How can we best represent it?

How will this representation tell us what we are looking for?

How do I communicate feedback to you?

Needs of the Teacher and Affirmations for Accomplishment

What anxieties are you experiencing?

How can I help you feel more comfortable?

Once again, what is it that you want me to look for?

How can I best communicate it to you following the lesson?

What would you like for me to do while the lesson is in progress?

What, if anything, can I do prior to the lesson?

Notes

1. Judith W. Little, "Seductive Images and Organizational Realities in Professional Development," in *Rethinking School Improvement: Research, Craft, and Concept*, ed. Ann Lieberman (New York: Teachers College Press, 1986).

2. Christopher Clark and Robert Yinger, "Teacher Planning," in *Exploring Teacher Thinking*, ed. James Calderhead (London: Cassell, 1987), pp. 84-103; Kathy Carter et al., "Processing and Using Information about Students: A Study of Expert, Novice and Postulant Teachers," *Teaching and Teacher Education* 3, no. 2 (1987): 147-57.

3. Louis Rubin, "The Thinking Teacher: Cultivating Pedagogical Intelligence," *Journal of Teacher Education* 40, no. 6 (1989): 31-34.

4. Barry K. Beyer, *Practical Strategies for the Teaching of Thinking* (Boston: Allyn & Bacon, 1987), p. 191.

5. Christopher M. Clark and Penelope L. Peterson, "Teachers' Thought Processes," in *Handbook of Research on Teaching*, 3rd ed., ed. Merlin C. Wittrock (New York: Macmillan, 1986), pp. 255-96; Robert J. Yinger, "A Study of Teacher Planning," *Elementary School Journal* 80, no. 3 (1980): 107-27.

6. Carol Livingston and Hilda Borko, "Expert-Novice Differences in Teaching: A Cognitive Analysis and Implications for Teacher Education," *Journal of Teacher Education* 40, no. 4 (1989): 36-42; Marylou Dantonio and James Randels, "Differences in Pedagogical Thought Processes Used in Planning, Conducting, and Reflecting by Novice and Experienced English Teachers" (paper presented at the annual conference of the Association of Teacher Educators, New Orleans, February 1991); Robert J. Yinger, "A Study of Teacher Planning."

7. Delores A. Westerman, "Expert and Novice Teacher Decision Making," *Journal of Teacher Education* 42, no. 4 (1991): 292-305.

8. Donald A. Schon, *Educating the Reflective Practitioner: Toward a New Design for Teaching and Learning in the Professions* (San Francisco: Jossey-Bass, 1987).

9. Livingston and Borko, "Expert-Novice Differences in Teaching"; Penelope L. Peterson and Michelle A. Comeaux, "Teachers' Schemata for Classroom Events: The Mental Scaffolding of Teachers' Thinking during Classroom Instruction," *Teaching and Teacher Education* 3, no. 4 (1987): 319-31; Robert J. Yinger, "Learning the Language of Practice," *Curriculum Inquiry* 17, no. 3 (1987): 293-318.

CHAPTER ELEVEN

Observation of Teaching Performance

The observation of teaching performance is an opportunity to learn about the effects of planned instruction. It is a time for the coaching partners to experiment with instructional practices and witness the results of the planning conference. It is an occasion for the coaching partners to gather information about content, students, and effective instructional delivery. Teachers have a chance to extend their understanding of content by using this experience to build on the development of a conceptual schema that serves to increase their understanding of the relationships between teaching and learning.[1]

During the observation, the coach collects specific, concrete information related to the observation focus that was determined by the coaching partners during the planning conference. The observation method and procedures discussed in the planning process are used to collect information that will assist the teacher in making decisions about her or his actual performance in presenting the lesson compared to what the teacher envisioned.

To provide a detailed account of the performance, the observation skills of the coach must be polished and sophisticated. The coach should be well versed in the use of observation tools and procedures. Observing instructional practices for the purpose of developing teaching talent requires that the coach be able to analyze lesson delivery as a sports coach analyzes plays of a game. The coach must know what to look for, how to look at it, and how to codify it so that it can be aptly communicated to the teacher. The more reliable and accurate the information, the more useful it is to the teacher in making decisions about refining instructional skills, techniques, and strategies.

Often the use of a tape recorder or video camera is beneficial in recording the lesson. The recorded lesson can be used by the coaching partners to stimulate reflection or to illustrate points of inquiry discussed during the debriefing conference. The teacher may want to hear or view the recording in order to focus on specific instructional skills or techniques. Recorded lessons serve as a series of snapshots of a teacher's journey into the professional development of the teaching self. These records also provide a portfolio of various teaching practices, illustrating the refinement of techniques and styles.

The data collected by the coach differs from that collected during teacher evaluation. Information gathered in a collegial coaching development process is—

- specific to the identified focus of observation determined by the coaching partners during the planning conference;
- recorded on instruments selected by or developed by the coaching partners in the planning conference;
- used to study specific teaching behaviors in the execution of a practice;
- kept confidential;
- presented to the teacher as a record of instructional events; and
- used as a springboard for reflecting on the personal, social, academic, and behavioral concerns of instruction in order to construct practical theories about instructional delivery.

Observation for the purpose of teacher evaluation has different assumptions and goals. Usually such observations are compiled into a cumulative record of service by an administrator responsible for evaluating teachers. The recorded observations represent evidence of a teacher's classroom performance as perceived by the evaluator. Information gathered in an evaluation process is—

- inclusive of all issues pertaining to instructional effectiveness;
- recorded on a standardized evaluation form;
- used to make judgments about a teacher's instructional delivery and effectiveness;
- kept in the teacher's permanent file for future reference in making decisions about retention, promotion, tenure, and merit;
- used to determine a teacher's strengths and weaknesses as perceived by the evaluator; and
- used to develop a remediation plan to improve instructional performance.

It is crucial to understand the distinctions between observations of a teacher's performance made by a coach and observations made by an evaluator. If teachers perceive that information gathered during the collegial coaching process will be used for purposes of evaluation, they may feel threatened and choose not to engage in future development activities. Therefore, the purpose for observing must be made clear and the data collected during the observation must remain with the coaching partners.

Any effort on the part of administrators to obtain the data will destroy the coaching partners' trust, confidence, and camaraderie. In turn, attempts to build a community of educators who are willing to experiment with instructional practices and build sound teaching repertoires that meet the needs of students will not occur. However, if administrators clearly delineate the boundaries of development and evaluation, both processes will contribute to sound educational practices for students.

Notes

1. Carol Livingston and Hilda Borko, "Expert-Novice Differences in Teaching: A Cognitive Analysis and Implications for Teacher Education," *Journal of Teacher Education* 40, no. 4 (1989): 36-42; Gaea Leinhardt, *Novice and Expert Knowledge of Individual Student's Achievement*, a report of research conducted by the Pennsylvania Learning Research and Development Center, University of Pittsburgh, for the National Institute of Education, Washington, D.C., 1983, ERIC No. ED 233 985; Gaea Leinhardt, "Math Lessons: A Contrast of Novice and Expert Competence," *Journal for Research in Mathematics Education* 20, no. 1 (1989): 52-75; Delores A. Westerman, "Expert and Novice Teacher Decision Making," *Journal of Teacher Education* 42, no. 4 (1991): 292-305.

CHAPTER TWELVE

Reflection Time

Reflection is the key activity of the collegial coaching process. Since teaching occurs in context, reflection provides time for the coaching partners to think about the relationship between the planned lesson and the observed performance. Through reflection, the coaching partners engage in teacher research concerning instruction and their performance in the classroom.[1] Thus, teachers build a practical theoretical framework that structures and informs their inquiry and decisions about classroom practice. Reflective time serves to challenge practices—why they are important, how they affect student learning, and what must change if they do not achieve the desired results with students.

Reflection requires that each teacher spend time alone thinking through the events of the lesson as it was conducted during the observation. Each partner records her or his thoughts in a journal, working out issues that will be shared in the subsequent debriefing conference. By spending 15 to 20 minutes after an observation writing down recollections, coaching partners create a valuable record of the teacher's development process. This record is called a *process portfolio*, an ongoing collection of teaching demonstrations, artifacts, and reflections about practices constructed by teachers throughout their professional growth and development.

Recording events of the lesson—for example, how the conducted lesson compared to the planned lesson, feelings and perceptions about the lesson, and how the lesson appeared to affect students—provides valuable information for solving instructional problems. Additionally, documentation of a teacher's introspection about his or her classroom performance is a process of self-assessment for measuring ongoing professional development. To reflect, the coaching partners must have enough time between the observation and the debriefing conference to contemplate perceptions recorded after the observation.

Reflecting on instructional experience plays a key role in teacher development. Dewey maintained that reflection is an important aspect of learning from experience. In discussing teacher development, he wrote that reflective thinking leads teachers to act in a "deliberate and intentional fashion" rather than in a "blind and impulsive" manner.[2] Experience for the sake of experience does not inform future instructional actions. In other words, how teachers think about or reflect on prior experiences influences subsequent instructional practices.

Karen Osterman defined reflection as "concentration and careful consideration" of what takes place during classroom instruction.[3] "Reflective practice is a professional development method which enables individual practitioners to become more skillful and more effective. . . . It leads to greater self-awareness, to development of new knowledge about professional practice, and to a broader understanding of the problems that confront practitioners."[4] The more opportunities teachers have to reflect on their instructional practices and to develop insights about the relationships between teaching and learning, the more skillful they can become in connecting their teaching to the outcomes of student learning.

Max Van Manen posits three levels of reflection.[5] The first converges on technical issues of practice. Here the teacher is concerned with the means rather than the results of instruction. Teachers focus their attention on how they are using skills such as questioning or classroom management. The question in the minds of teachers is, How do I use the technique?

At Van Manen's second level of reflection, a teacher's values are the basis for decision making. Teachers ask, What do I believe about this particular instructional practice? All educational choices and actions, Van Manen theorizes, have their roots in the individual teacher's ability to interpret actions and events. Teachers' values will ultimately determine what they will do and how they will perform. If teachers believe that children learn best through a hands-on approach, they will tend to use methods and practices that incorporate hands-on instruction. However, if teachers believe that children learn best through lecture, they will unlikely change their instructional approach to accommodate hands-on instruction, even if mandated to do so.

Van Manen's third level of reflection centers on issues of the worth of knowledge and social conditions. It is at this level that teachers consider the relationships between instructional practices and learning outcomes. They ask, In what way will this instructional practice impact the development of student knowledge, attitudes, and skills? When teachers reflect on the value of knowledge and the social conditions inherent in a learning context, they are more likely to change their instructional practices and broaden their instructional repertoires to include new ones.

For example, let us assume that a teacher believes that lecture is a sound method of instruction, and she has used it effectively for years. But reflecting about the low achievement of a certain group of learners, the teacher explores possible reasons more deeply. The teacher may begin to question the relationship between his or her instructional methods and learner outcomes. For contentious teachers, this will probably lead to experimentation with different instructional practices.

Experimentation occurs not because the teacher has changed his or her values or beliefs. The teacher experiments with alternative instructional practices to ascertain the effects they might have on learning. Adaptations are made based on the teacher's perceptions. It is important to note that Donald Schon argues that teachers must go beyond the level of technical reflection, because "the problems of real-world practice do not present themselves to practitioners as well-formed structures."[6] In time, given different students and social and educational events, what works and does not work often eludes established routines and practices.

Teaching is contextual; any application of technique or strategy must be examined in light of this fact. Each invitation to teach requires that teachers adjust their instructional practices to meet the needs of individual students. By collaborating, the coaching partners have an opportunity to share their insights, resolve instructional dilemmas, and become more confident about which instructional practices work and why.

Throughout the collegial coaching cycle, the coaching partners are constantly engaged in thinking about their lesson plans, the effects particular instructional practices have on student participation and learning, and the conditions necessary for specific learning outcomes. In this way, they become more certain about the effectiveness of their instructional practices.

Teacher Efficacy

Of all the issues that confront teachers in their professional development, none is more important than their sense of efficacy, that is, their power to produce an effect. Patricia Ashton defines this as "the extent to which teachers believe that they have the capacity to affect student behavior."[7] The concept of teacher efficacy is grounded in Albert Bandura's theory of self-efficacy.[8] He believes that "efficacy expectations are a major determinant of people's choice of activities, how much effort they will expend, and of how long they will sustain effort in dealing with stressful situations."[9] Thomas Guskey categorizes teacher efficacy as general and personal: "Teachers may believe that certain practices or teaching behaviors will affect student performance (general) but, at the same time, may not believe that they can perform those necessary activities (personal)."[10] For example, a teacher believes strongly that critical questioning develops students' critical thinking skills, but, lacking the knowledge or skills to conduct strategic lessons using effective questioning processes, she or he asks recall questions instead. Because the teacher does not trust that she or he is competent to instruct students to think more critically, she or he continues practices that are comfortable.

The collegial coaching process assists teachers in understanding what they want students to accomplish and what teaching behaviors they must possess in order for students to attain the desired outcomes of the lesson. Insights about the relationship between teaching practices and learner achievements are developed in the process. Thus, teachers' attitudes about efficacy are more likely reflected in their instructional practices and students' level of achievement.[11] In other words, what teachers believe and value tends to be what they do in practice.

When Susan Rosenholtz studied teachers' workplaces, she discovered that "when teachers collectively perceive students as capable learners and themselves as capable teachers vested with a technical culture to help them learn and grow, they seem more likely to persevere, to define problem students as a challenge, to seek outside resources to conquer that challenge, and, in this way, to actually foster students' academic gains."[12] Thus, the more confidence teachers have, the more adept they are at using a variety of instructional practices effectively. Likewise, the more teachers know about the relationship between instruction and learning, the greater the likelihood that they will explore, inquire into, and apply successful instructional practices in the classroom. When teachers engage in collaborative professional development, however, reflection may result in less certainty about the effectiveness of a particular practice or their ability to perform successfully.[13] As teachers become more knowledgeable about issues and practices, it is not uncommon for them to question the validity of comfortable practices.

This rethinking and consequent lack of certainty may cause teachers to feel disconcerted for a time. As one teacher expressed it, "What happens in coaching is that everything you do is questioned. Nothing has any boundaries now. You're constantly reassessing what you're doing. It's not like the courses you had in teacher education where everything could be tied up in a nice, pretty red bow. All of a sudden you're not sure about anything, because, rather than just doing something, you are constantly trying to make sense of what you do."

In a sense, coaching is like a Salitsky dot image system, a field of seemingly random points of color from which a three-dimensional image can be distinguished. The more one gazes at the field of dots, the more depth and clarity appear. The image that was at first hidden becomes a whole new way of seeing. Such is the case when teachers engage in collegial coaching. Studying teaching opens teachers' eyes to the depth and enchantment of instructional processes.

Challenging preconceived notions about teaching and learning must be viewed as a positive step towards development. It reminds us of the old adage that the more you know, the more you realize you don't know. To resolve this dilemma, teachers must be given sufficient time to reflect on lessons, to collaborate with others, and to experiment with instructional practices in order to determine for themselves the impact of various instructional practices.

Reflection provides a compelling opportunity for teachers to think about their techniques and experiences. And when teachers record thoughts from their reflections, they create a self-portrait of their professional growth. As teachers become more familiar with the details of instructional implementation, they can develop expertise in reflective practice. Reflective practice in teaching has the potential to inspire judicious experimentation that leads to more certainty about effective instruction. As teachers better understand the inner workings of instructional practices and gain confidence in applying and adapting these to different classroom situations, they develop teaching repertoires that more aptly address student learning needs. Collegial coaching facilitates teacher efficacy in that teachers learn to assess themselves critically as evolving teachers through reflecting on and recording their instructional development.

Reflection Time Question Guide

Lesson Purpose

What was the intent of the lesson?
Why is it important to students?
What will students gain from this lesson?
How will it impact their thinking, their attitudes, or their abilities?
What reasons exist for these beliefs?

Teacher Development

How effectively did the teacher use the instructional practices?
What was performed well?
What needs further development?

Effects on Students

In what ways do the practices employed enhance student learning?
What basis is there for believing this?
In what ways do the practices employed distract from the intended learning outcomes?
What could be changed to better meet the needs of students or achieve the lesson outcomes?
What reasons do I have for believing these changes will better meet the needs of students or achieve the learning outcomes?

Collaborative Communications

Which of the issues are most important?
Why are they important?
What will be my coaching partner's reaction to these issues?
How can I describe these reflections to my coaching partner during the debriefing conference?

Notes

1. F. Michael Connelly and D. Jean Clandinin, *Teachers as Curriculum Planners: Narratives of Experience* (New York: Teachers College Press, 1988).

2. John Dewey, *Experience and Education* (New York: Macmillan, 1938), p. 17.

3. Karen F. Osterman, "Reflective Practice: A New Agenda for Education," *Education and Urban Society* 22, no. 2 (1990): 132-52.

4. Ibid., p. 134.

5. Max Van Manen, "Linking Ways of Knowing with Ways of Being Practical," *Curriculum Inquiry* 6, no. 3 (1977): 205-28.

6. Donald A. Schon, *Educating the Reflective Practitioner: Toward a New Design for Teaching and Learning in the Professions* (San Francisco: Jossey-Bass, 1987), p. 4.

7. Patricia T. Ashton, "Teacher Efficacy: A Motivational Paradigm for Effective Teacher Education," *Journal of Teacher Education* 35, no. 5 (1984): 28.

8. Albert Bandura, "Self-Efficacy: Toward a Unifying Theory of Behavioral Change," *Psychological Review* 84, no. 2 (1977): 191-215.

9. Ibid., p. 194.

10. Thomas R. Guskey, "Context Variables That Affect Measures of Teacher Efficacy," *Journal of Educational Research* 81, no. 1 (1987): 41.

11. Ashton, "Teacher Efficacy."

12. Susan J. Rosenholtz, *Teachers' Workplace: The Social Organization of Schools* (New York: Longman, 1989), p. 138.

13. Elizabeth Broom, "A Study of Peer Coaching and the Relationship between Teacher Efficacy and Stages of Concern" (Ph.D. diss., University of New Orleans, 1994); John A. Ross, "Teacher Efficacy and the Effects of Coaching on Student Achievement," *Canadian Journal of Education* 17, no. 1 (1992): 51-65.

CHAPTER THIRTEEN

Debriefing Conference

The debriefing conference is a forum for problem solving. The substance of the conference grows out of reflection on the lesson's implementation. It is an avenue for comparing preparation with performance in the classroom. In the debriefing conference, the coaching partners collaborate to create an action plan for assuring instructional effectiveness. They identify teaching strengths and deficiencies as well as unmet goals of instruction. It is a time for sharing reflections on the conducted lesson and initiating the delineation of future instructional events. Reflection plays a key role in empowering the coaching partners to be deliberate and insightful during this problem-solving conference.[1]

The coaching partners concentrate their efforts on identifying teaching techniques, skills, or processes that were successful and those that need improvement. The sharing of insights about the discrepancies between the planned lesson and the teacher's conduct of the lesson becomes the basis for solving instructional enigmas. The coach assists the teacher in solving instructional problems by asking probing questions. The questions should facilitate the teacher's understanding of the issues related to instruction, the necessary conditions for implementing successful instructional activities, and the consequences of the interplay between teacher actions and student learning. To do so, the coach establishes a pattern of questioning that alternates between what? and why?

The debriefing conference can be as short as five minutes or as long as one-half hour. The longer conferences should be reserved for novice teachers, since they will need more attention in solving problems and analyzing lesson implementation. Novice teachers ordinarily do not have sufficient experience to form insights or to draw conclusions about instructional problems confronting them in the classroom. When coaching teachers have attained some degree of teaching expertise, the debriefing conference need only attend to precise issues related to refinements in technique. Often, more expert teachers know what they need to do to improve their instructional efforts; however, by participating in the collegial coaching cycle, they confirm their teaching strengths and better understand themselves as developing teachers.

Following the analysis of the teaching performance, a question guide is used to assist the coaching partners in problem solving (see page 84). Like the planning conference, in order for the questions to make sense to the teacher, the coach needs to attend carefully to the teacher's responses, clarifying any vague remarks. The order and sequence of the questions provides a framework for exploring solutions related to the delivery of instruction. More than likely, the coach will need to adjust the phrasing, appropriateness, and sequence of the questions in order to accommodate the teacher's thinking process.

The goals of the planning and debriefing conferences are different. Whereas the planning conference is a time to establish the problem focus of the lesson and prepare the teacher for the instructional event, the debriefing conference is an occasion to explore potential ways of eliminating discrepancies between what was anticipated and what actually occurred during instruction. As the debriefing conference unfolds, the coaching partners share ideas, discuss goals, and deliberate on the teacher's techniques that are strong and ones to be developed. Throughout their dialogue, they focus on developing expertise in instructional skills, techniques, and strategies used in the lesson, paying particular attention to the issue specified for observation during the planning conference. They also explore the basis for using various instructional practices and how these affected student participation during the lesson.

The debriefing conference is comparable to the post-conference of the clinical supervision process. However, one major difference is the span of time between the observation and the follow-up conference. In clinical supervision, the supervisor or administrator and the teacher get together immediately following the observation to discuss the lesson and evaluate the teacher's instructional efforts.[2] In the collegial coaching cycle, the debriefing conference occurs after each of the coaching partners has had sufficient time to reflect on the lesson and discern the differences between what the teacher planned and the actual events of instruction. This pause is important, since coaching is a developmental process, not an evaluative one. The coaching partners need time to develop insights about teaching and learning. Additionally, the goal of the collegial coaching processes is to assist teachers in becoming more reflective about their teaching practices. In becoming more reflective, teachers are more likely to test out practices and, in turn, build style and technique in the delivery of instruction.

The debriefing conference has three distinct problem-solving steps. Like the planning conference, these steps appear linear; however, in practice they merge. The instructional issues that need to be discussed by the coaching partners are:

- statement of discrepancies,
- analysis of teaching actions, and
- generation of solutions and effects.

Statement of Discrepancies

The debriefing conference commences as the coach focuses the discussion on what the teacher envisioned would happen during the lesson. This anchors the discussion and draws out issues that surface as a result of comparing the lesson plan and the lesson implementation. Questions that stimulate this dialogue are, What did you expect to happen in the lesson? and, What did you plan to do in this lesson? The focus of the observation of the teaching performance is reviewed. The coach may ask the teacher what the focus was or may simply state it, depending on how direct or indirect the coach wants to be.

Subsequently, the coach asks the teacher to recall what actually transpired during the lesson, and the coaching partners investigate their perceptions of the differences between what was supposed to happen and what actually happened. The coach's questioning concentrates on the discrepancies between planning and performing, emphasizing the teacher's reasoning processes. The concluding questions blend the teacher's practical knowledge, attained through experience conducting the lesson, with known theories of teaching and learning. The goal of the debriefing conference is for the coaching partners to uncover the cause-effect relationships between teaching actions and student learning.

The following series of questions is important in deriving the practice/theory relationship of the instructional events: What issues would you like to focus on? Why do you want to focus on these issues? What do you hope to gain from our discussion? How will this assist you in your instructional development? In what way was conducting the lesson different from what you anticipated? What was different about your actions? What were you thinking about? Why did you change from your original plan? What in students' actions was different from what you anticipated? Why do you think the students responded in this manner?

Analysis of Teaching Actions

The primary purpose for engaging in collegial coaching is to develop the instructional talents of teachers. To make this happen, the coaching partners must focus their attention on strengths and areas to be developed in the teacher's instructional repertoire. Nothing will change until the teacher comes to terms with what needs to be changed, why it needs to be changed, and how it can be changed. This is based on a teacher's ability to internalize debriefing conference discussions, previously referred to as "self-vision."

Self-vision involves developing a discriminating eye for discrepancies between how a teacher pictures herself or himself teaching and what actually occurs. The ability to see oneself in action can make a direct contribution to the development of certainty about teaching practices and the effects specific teaching practices have on student learning. Donald Schon uses the phrase "reflection in action" to describe teachers' perceptions of themselves as they teach.[3] As teachers focus on their delivery, they make adjustments to their instruction. The coach is instrumental in helping the teacher acquire this ability. Until the teacher can reflect in action, the coach is the mirror of the teaching self.[4]

Once teaching and learning issues are discerned, the coach can focus the conference on teaching behaviors. This is done to spotlight practices the teacher should keep or develop as he or she continues to deliver instruction. Keep in mind that this is not an evaluation of teaching performance, but a sharing of ideas about perceptions gleaned from the observation.

To focus the discussion, the coach asks the teacher for observations and reflections about his or her performance in the classroom, alternating between what? and why? questions to assist the teacher in becoming more inquisitive about his or her instructional efforts. Such a sequence of questions might include, What did you feel you did well during the lesson? Why do you think it was necessary for you to do that? What were you having difficulty with? Why do you think that was difficult or not handled as effectively as you would have liked? These questions afford opportunities for teachers to rethink their performance of the lesson. Following the teacher's responses, the coach shares his or her insights and provides support for the teacher's perceptions by citing personal examples or evidence from educational theories.

Keep in mind that strengths and areas of development are discussed and explored because they are important to the coached teacher's refinement of technique and style. Teachers will be more likely to identify solutions or changes in teaching behaviors if they feel that they own the analysis of their performance.

Generation of Solutions and Effects

Exploring solutions to instructional problems and unsettling practices requires the coaching partners to be resourceful. Solutions can be derived through prior teaching experiences, workshops, books, and observations of other teachers' practices. Experimentation with various teaching practices is key to developing effective ones. Both coaching partners must be risk takers, open to examining and experimenting with new practices. They must study the effects of practices in various instructional contexts and be willing to adopt ones that work and throw out ones that do not serve the learning environment.

Questions to assist teachers in exploring solutions that enhance classroom instruction include: In what way was the evolving situation or experience problematic for you? Why did this bother you? What do you think you should do to change? If you change, what do you think will result in terms of students, you, and future instructional events? Why is this change important to you? How do you plan to implement this? What problems do you think you will have? Why? What benefits will be derived from this change? What makes you think these benefits will result from implementing this change?

Maintaining effective instructional practices is as important as changing ineffective ones. Insights about teaching strengths must be explored and nurtured or they soon will disappear. To help the teacher focus on techniques, strategies, or practices that should be maintained, the coach can ask questions such as: What techniques or practices would you like to maintain? Why would you like to maintain these? How do you think these practices impact your classroom performance?

In concluding the debriefing conference, the coach may want to address how the teacher has changed her or his thinking about instruction as a result of the inquiry into instructional practices. Additionally, the coach may query the teacher about practices for future study. The following questions may be useful to that end: How do you think these practices will impact your thinking about instruction, student learning, and future goals for developing your teaching repertoire? What do you want to focus on next time we meet? When would you like to meet?

In summary, the debriefing conference is problem focused, requiring teachers to solve dilemmas about their teaching practices uncovered during their reflections. The conference must be perceived as a risk-free environment wherein teachers discuss problems related to technique and style as well as explore pertinent issues about the effects of their practices on student learning. At first the conference may make teachers feel uncomfortable, since it places the responsibility for development on them. As teachers become more comfortable with the conference format and process, they will begin to feel more in control of their teaching selves and more confident in the delivery of alternative instructional practices. The debriefing conference offers the coaching partners freedom to inquire, experiment, and solve problems emerging in various instructional contexts.

Debriefing Conference Question Guide

Statement of Discrepancies
    What did you expect to happen in the lesson?
        What did you plan to do in the lesson?
    What actually happened when you conducted the lesson?
    What issues would you like to focus on?
        Why do you want to focus on these issues?
        What do you hope to gain from our discussion?
        How will this assist you in your instructional development?
    In what way was conducting the lesson different from what you anticipated?
        What was different about your actions?
        What were you thinking about?
        Why did you change from your original plan?
    What was different in the student actions from what you anticipated?
        Why do you think the students responded in this manner?

Analysis of Teaching Actions
    What did you feel you did well during the lesson?
        Why do you think it was necessary for you to do that?
    What were you having difficulty with?
        Why do you think that was difficult or not handled as effectively as you would have liked?

Generation of Solutions and Effects
    In what way was the situation or experience problematic for you as it evolved?
        Why did this bother you?
    What do you think you should do to change?
        If you change, what do you think will result in terms of students, you, and future instructional events?
        Why is this change important to you?
    How do you plan to implement this change?
    What problems do you think you will have? Why?
    What benefits will be derived from this change?
    What makes you think these benefits will result from implementing this change?
    What techniques or practices would you like to maintain?
        Why would you like to maintain them?
    How do you think these practices impact your classroom performance?
    How do you think these practices will impact your thinking about instruction, student learning, and your future goals for developing your teaching repertoire?
    What do you want to focus on next time we meet?
    When would you like to meet?

Notes

1. Donald A. Schon, "Coaching Reflective Teaching," in *Reflection in Teacher Education*, ed. Peter P. Grimmett and Gaalen L. Erickson (New York: Teachers College Press, 1988).

2. Robert H. Anderson and Karolyn J. Snyder, eds. *Clinical Supervision: Coaching for Higher Performance* (Lancaster, Penn.: Technomic Publishing Company, 1993).

3. Donald A. Schon, *Educating the Reflective Practitioner: Toward a New Design for Teaching and Learning in the Professions* (San Francisco: Jossey-Bass, 1987).

4. Pamela Robbins, *How to Plan and Implement a Peer Coaching Program* (Alexandria, Va.: Association for Supervision and Curriculum Development, 1991).

Part Three
Collegial Inquiry

CHAPTER FOURTEEN

Professional Inquiry and Collegial Self-Study

Excellence is recognizable to most people. To fully appreciate its magnificence, however, one must study how it got there. Then you feel the tingle.

—Jane Alexander, chair, National Endowment for the Arts

Inquiry into the teaching self demands that educators be able to observe and analyze instruction from a variety of perspectives. While it is important that we understand how children learn, it is equally important that we understand ourselves as teachers and recognize our capacities to learn how we approach excellence in our teaching. Professional inquiry into our teaching provides us with information to make professional judgments about those problems and achievements that concern our instruction. Our reflections on our instructional experiences allow us to relive these events from a distance and reconsider them with understandings and insights subsequent to our instructional performance. Sharing with other educators our instructional experiences and what we have learned as professionals nurtures and shapes our collective impressions, notions, insights, and knowledge about teaching and learning.

What happens to us in the classroom influences our assumptions, values, beliefs, knowledge, and learning about teaching: our recollections of our teaching experiences accelerate our learning and deeply influence who we are becoming as educators and how we perform in the classroom. Our reflections signal what else we must know, what other techniques we need to acquire, and what information we must collect about our students to refine our professional judgments. When we do this with groups of other caring educators, we evolve practice theories that are based in our teaching situations, our instructional contexts. Our teaching experiences, our reflections on them, and our sharing of practice theories are the catalysts and guides for further inquiry and study of successful contextual instructional performances.

I use the word "performance" in terms of conducting lessons with students to effect student learning. I use the word "practice" in reference to what teachers do to learn about instructional delivery. I use these words for two reasons; one has to do with school realities, the other with my belief that when we teach we are performing artists. Performing artists learn their craft by preparing; by rehearsing under varying conditions; by reviewing the performance; by analyzing what the "self" did with the audience in order to refine the performance. Learning to teach professionally means practicing one's craft and getting it right for the performance. It's what artists refer to as "practicing their craft." They are studying it to get better at doing it.

In reality, little time is built into school schedules for teachers to "practice" their craft. Together we are the practice (a noun), but we do not practice (the verb). We are always with learners or planning to be with learners. Preparing usually means we are getting our materials or equipment ready. Our lessons with our students are simultaneously rehearsal and performance. Infrequently, if ever, are we afforded the luxury on school time to meet with other educators about our thoughts on our lessons, to share our reflections about our instructional experiences, to practice specific techniques and processes in a systematic manner, or to share what we have learned with other educators who care. Rarely are we afforded time for ongoing dialogue and study to inform our everyday performances. If anything, we call what we do every day "teaching practice," as though the only way we can learn and should learn about instructional practice is through years and years of practice only—never delivering the performance.

If we are serious about student learning and implementing quality practices, then we have no choice but to understand and conduct exemplary learning experiences. This idea is not new to our profession. Educators throughout the twentieth century understood this about teacher development.[1] Why are we still "in practice," mostly trying to find school time to study teaching as professionals? When will we understand that inquiry into teaching and collegial sharing of our teaching practices *is* teaching? When will we invite teacher learning to become a focus in our professional work?

Inquiry into instruction in collegial self-study forums can serve to expedite learning for all educators involved in the processes. To study teaching through inquiry and collegial self-study involves learning about teaching in the manner other performing artists learn their craft. They pick it apart and put it back together, forming impressions, creating assumptions, perfecting skills and techniques, reflecting on all and sharing their insights with other trusted artists. They analyze to create excellence in their performances.

By analyzing how our instruction is generated and performed, we afford ourselves opportunities to become competent, capable of comprehending instructional excellence. To be aptly conscious of ourselves as practitioners brings us closer to effecting quality instruction. We can share the intricacies of our instructional techniques and methods with other caring educators, and we can systematically collect information about our instructional performances. Deborah Ball and David Cohen call this a "pedagogy of professional development" in the school context.[2] They propose that professional knowledge arises from investigating our pedagogical assumptions and practices and that this inquiry is a key element in a professional approach to learning. In other words, inquiry into the analysis of instructional actions requires us to examine our beliefs, assumptions, and values about learning and our teaching practices and to do something about it during classroom performances.

Similarly, Michael Connely and Jean Clandini refer to "personal practical knowledge . . . a moral, affective, and aesthetic way of knowing life's educational situations."[3] Inquiry-centered approaches for professional development provide an avenue for practitioners to engage in building contextual knowledge about their instructional practices and learners.[4] Marilyn Cochran-Smith and Susan Lytle point out that pedagogical knowledge is developed synergistically, from "outside-in" and "inside-out."[5] Simply put, how educators learn about instructional knowledge does not just flow from researcher to teacher. Pedagogical knowledge also is formed, framed, and flows from teacher to researcher as K-12 practitioners engage in systematic analysis of classroom practice.

In her writings on self-study research, Jean McNiff insists that teachers develop personal theories about education by drawing upon their own experiences.[6] Donald Schon calls these experiences "reflection in action."[7] James Calderhead and Peter Gates posit that "[t]he current enthusiasm for reflective teaching may be partly explained in terms of an attempt to understand more fully what is distinctive about teachers' professional development and to come to terms with its complexity."[8]

Reflective practice engages teachers in efforts to critically examine their classroom performance in order to develop a more sophisticated awareness about their actions in the context of instruction.[9] Karen Oesterman and Robert Kottkamp remind us that reflective practice is about us and that we are the bottom line when it comes to initiating organizational change.[10] Reflective practice is an opportunity for caring educators to examine carefully the contextual situations arising from classroom instruction and to take action to understand the conditions necessary for our personal instructional excellence.

Through this contemplation, we have the potential to monitor our assumptions about instruction, learning, and teaching, as well as influence our practice in a healthy manner. Concomitantly, as Ardra Cole and Gary Knowles point out, we filter what we know about teaching and learning through our understanding of ourselves.[11] In writing about ongoing professional development, they assert that teaching is inquiry framed by our beliefs, experiences, and values. "Engaging in research on one's own teaching and being reflexive about one's professional practice are one and the same when the inquiry begins with and returns to the teaching self."[12] Our teaching selves are shaped by what we understand of our learning selves. Both influence our instructional practices with students.

While the starting place for school reform and instructional renewal begins with each of us, to sustain it we must move beyond ourselves and cultivate communities of collegial inquiry that study and research teaching. Teachers uniting together to reflect upon and inquire into the improvement or enhancement of instruction is honorable work. It is worthy of the time needed for such experiences. Susan Rosenhholtz finds clear, positive connections between increased teacher learning time and success in student learning in her research on schools as a social organization.[13] To shape the quality of instructional experiences for learners in context requires collegial self-study.

Collegial self-study is an interdependent approach for reflecting upon our practice knowledge while helping other educators reflect upon their practice to more completely understand it. Donald Schon refers to this as "collective inquiry."[14] To engage in collegial self-study results in sharing insights and illuminations to build professional cultures and to define, contextually, our assumptions about excellence in teaching and our effect on student learning. After all, inquiries into our assumptions and actions as educators create the portraits of who we are as learning professionals and influence our educational judgments. Our collegial self-study assists us in acquiring insights into how the learning process evolves for our students and ourselves and how we connect instructional theory and practice to our own professional development. Thus, we develop theories of practice. Lev Vygotsky's theory that learners have the potential to learn more when they work with others is not confined to children.[15] School renewal cannot occur through self-study alone, however. The confluence of self-study and collegial inquiry is central to learning about our teaching selves.

Collegial self-study has the potential to enlighten the way we think about teaching and learning, to characterize the manner in which we practice teaching, and to influence our instructional judgments. While its impetus comes from engaging in personal reflective practice, collegial self-study asks us to share our understandings with other reflective practitioners. In doing so, we create communities of inquiry that contribute to strengthening our theories of learning in the context of our practice and sensitize our awareness of and precision in delivering quality instruction. Through these connections, we are afforded greater opportunities to learn more about ourselves as learners and as teachers. It is a synergistic process that generates new ways of thinking about instruction and inspires a revitalization of professional practice in all who participate.

Thus, the scope of the original conceptualization of collegial coaching is extended to include not only coaching partners but also collegial self-study groups. The agency of the group is to experiment with instruction, to inquire into the nature of instructional processes and products, and to share the group's contextual findings as a means for improving, supporting, and generating effective instructional practices. It is based on and in concert with warranted assumptions, beliefs, and understandings of classroom practice.

Collegial self-study fosters the notion that professional development is both cognitive and social in nature. Collegial coaching, whether carried out as a partnership or as a collegial self-study group, possesses one unifying premise: Teacher development is reflective in nature. It is collaborative; learning occurs though social dialogue. Experimentation with and investigations into instruction are teacher initiated, teacher sponsored, and teacher driven.

Notes

1. Linda Darling-Hammond and Gary Sykes, eds., *Teaching As the Learning Profession: Handbook of Policy and Practice* (San Francisco: Jossey-Bass,1999).

2. Deborah L. Ball and David K. Cohen, "Developing Practice, Developing Practitioners: a Practice-Based Theory of Professional Education," in *Teaching As the Learning Profession: Handbook of Policy and Practice*, ed. Linda Darling-Hammond and Gary Sykes (San Francisco: Jossey-Bass, 1999), pp. 3-32.

3. F. Michael Connelly and D. Jean Clandinin, *Teachers as Curriculum Planners: Narrative of Experience* (New York: Teachers College Press, 1988).

4. Glenda L. Bissex and Richard H. Bullock, *Seeing for Ourselves: Case Study Research by Teachers of Writing* (Portsmouth, N.H.: Heinemann, 1987); D. Dixie Goswami and Peter Stillman, *Reclaiming the Classroom: Teacher Research As an Agency for Change* (Upper Montclair, N.J.: Boynton/Cook, 1987); Marion M. Mohr and Marions Maclean, *Working Together: A Guide for Teacher-Researchers* (Urbana, Ill.: National Council of Teachers of English, 1987).

5. Marilyn Cochran-Smith and Susan L. Lytle, *Inside/Outside: Teacher Research and Knowledge* (New York: Teachers College Press, 1993).

6. Jean McNiff, *Teaching As Learning: An Action Research Approach* (London: Routledge Press, 1993); and Jean McNiff, *You and Your Action Research* (London: Routledge Press, 1996). See also, Jack Whitehead, "Creating a Living Educational Theory from Questions of the Kind, 'How Do I Improve My Practice?'" *Cambridge Journal of Education* 19, no.1 (1989): 41-52.

7. Donald A. Schon, *Educating the Reflective Practitioner* (San Francisco: Jossey-Bass, 1987).

8. James Calderhead and Peter Gates, "Introduction," in *Conceptualizing Reflection in Teacher Development*, ed. J. James Calderhead and Peter Gates (London: Falmer Press, 1993), p. 1.

9. Wilfred Carr and Stephen Kemmis, *Becoming Critical: Education, Knowledge and Action Research* (London: Falmer Press, 1986).

10. Karen F. Osterman and R. Robert B. Kottkamp, *Reflective Practice for Educators: Improving Schooling Through Professional Development* (Newbury Park, Calif.: Corwin Press, 1993).

11. Ardra L. Cole and J. Gary Knowles, *Researching Teaching: Exploring Teacher Development Through Reflexive Inquiry* (Boston: Allyn & Bacon, 2000).

12. Ibid., p. 94.

13. Susan J. Rosenholtz, *Teacher's Workplace: The Social Organization of Schools* (New York: Teachers College Press, 1991).

14. Schon, *Educating the Reflective Practitioner*.

15. Lev S. Vygotsky, *Mind in Society: The Development of Higher Psychological Process*, ed. Michael Cole et al. (Cambridge, Mass.: Harvard University Press, 1978).

CHAPTER FIFTEEN

Collegial Analysis Self-Study Support Teams (CASSST)

At its core, team learning is a discipline of practices designed, over time, to get the people of the team thinking and acting together. The team members do not need to think alike. . . . [T]hrough regular practice, they can learn to be effective in concert.

—Peter Senge,
Schools That Learn

In the last chapter, I spoke of the importance of inquiry and collegial self-study. In this chapter, I discuss how the collegial coaching process can be used by teams of teachers to study instructional processes. John Dewey believed that educational enlightenment comes from contributing ideas from one's experiences and that sharing our individual ideas in concert with each other affects the quality of learning for all.[1] Using the collegial coaching cycle to inquire into the conditions of our instruction and the effects our practices have on learners can clarify our understanding of exemplary instruction within our own educational contexts.

For me personally, the importance of teacher inquiry has been best realized through my work with teachers in studying questioning practices. My ongoing investigations into the nature and function of question-answer interactions has helped me attend to the significance of collegial dialogue in refining teaching talent. Peter Senge underscores the significance of dialogue among colleagues:

> During the dialogue process, people learn how to think together—not just in the sense of analyzing a shared problem or creating new pieces of shared knowledge but in the sense of occupying a collective sensibility, in which the thoughts, emotions, and resulting actions belong not to one individual, but to all of them together.[2]

Whether our collegial self-study of teaching practices focuses on adding new techniques to our repertoire or refining familiar ones, dialogue on and rehearsals of specific techniques are valuable means for acquiring excellence in our teaching performances. Reflection and collegial dialogue are central ingredients for stimulating growth-in-practice. Equally important is the notion of growth-through-practice, as I mentioned earlier. To grow through practice as other performing artists do, we must also engage in diverse types of rehearsals. Rehearsals permit us safe opportunities to collect information about our instruction, reflect upon our delivery, and engage in self-analysis to determine the effects of our teaching on learners. We also have the responsibility to collaborate with other caring, trusted classroom educators in order to come to collective understandings about excellence in instruction.

In *Learning to Question, Questioning to Learn*, I embrace more fully the metaphor of teaching as a performing art to describe a growth-through-practice approach to teacher learning:

> Teaching is a performing art. Like other performing art fields, such as acting, music, or gymnastics, the talents of performers must be developed and refined through a nurturing process that integrates practice and reflection upon practice. This reflective practice process becomes a means for developing technique and style. For practice and reflection to become reflective practice, the nurturing of talents first requires that performers possess a mental picture of what the perfected practice looks like in a well-executed performance. Secondly, reflective practice requires that performers study the practice(s) by observing carefully aspects of their execution of the technique in practice situations while constantly analyzing and measuring their execution of the technique against their internal vision of a well-implemented lesson within a performance situation.[3]

To inquire into instructional practices using a performing arts model requires types of rehearsals that permit us to observe and to reflect upon our instructional practices. Collegial rehearsals have the potential to reinforce the formation and execution of exemplary instructional practices. The collegial coaching cycle is a useful process for cultivating our collegial conversations about development and refinement of teaching practice. By using the collegial coaching cycle, we can engage in self-study and share what we learn with other classroom educators in a systematic and structured manner. Collegial self-study can serve to inform our theories about teaching and learning within the context of our school settings.

Collegial self-study allows us to observe our teaching performances more precisely, analyze them more carefully through reflective practice, and dialogue more consistently in order to understand exemplary instructional practices in context. While the self-study of our instructional practices may be investigated alone, empowerment of our teaching selves can be heightened through studying our teaching practices collectively. Inquiry into our instruction using a collegial self-study approach allows teachers to collaborate in planning, observing, and analyzing both troublesome and successful techniques though systematic and continual rehearsals. Collegial rehearsals free educators to think about the process of instruction and internalize techniques without the constraint of being responsible for student learning.

Collegial self-study and collegial rehearsals provide classroom educators the luxury of practicing, observing, and analyzing instructional techniques and strategies while in safe, analytical settings prior to integrating them in a classroom context where quality of instruction is important in achieving results with students. Permitting ourselves time to practice prior to and subsequent to our classroom performances has the power to influence our thinking and actions during instruction.

To amplify our understanding of our own instructional practices, often we need reflective advice and continued support from trusted, caring colleagues. Our trusted colleagues can be sounding boards for our ideas, other lenses through which we develop our understandings of the instructional process, critics who ask us tough questions that inspire and challenge us to accept new inquiries about our own and our students' learning processes. While one-on-one coaching is a safe haven for sharing insights about our instructional efforts, the merger of the collegial coaching process with collegial self-study invites opportunities for us to engage in more critical thought about what we believe quality instruction is. It also can contribute to how effectively we carry out our instructional beliefs in classroom practice. Additionally, our collective curiosity about instruction and professional development leads us into collaborating more with each other in investigating perplexing educational issues and practices that arise from professional dialogue. The generation of practice-based theory by educators who commonly own their understandings about teaching and learning and who view instruction as problematic and contextual can influence significantly the learning of the students they serve.

The CASSST

In keeping with the metaphor of teaching as a performing art, I refer to educators who come together for the purposes of generating knowledge and seasoning skills, while supporting each others' professional learning through inquiry, as "the CASSST" Collegial Analysis Self-Study Support Team. CASSST members are teachers who regularly collaborate to inquire into teaching practices. They develop, conduct, document, and critique their performances. They refine instructional techniques, solve common instructional problems, and look critically at the relationships between teaching and learning. As a team, they generate theories about instruction that emerge from their study of practice. They evolve common visions of the context in which they deliver instruction and are enlightened about how students are profiting or stagnating from the use of particular instructional practices. Likewise, the CASSST strives to identify changes that need to be made in the curriculum or instructional practices that better match the learning needs, concerns, and styles of students.

The CASSST consists of a small group of teachers. An even number is important in case the team decides to engage in coaching. The CASSST is a professional learning community that safeguards opportunities for rehearsing instruction. Members of the team do not evaluate each other during their rehearsals or performances; rather, they use the phases of the collegial coaching cycle to share ideas about expert instruction. Refining teaching in this manner is a reflective, skill-acquisition process and not simply the memorization of information. Teachers cannot learn to teach by reading about it or studying it. They must practice it in diverse rehearsal situations and reflect upon and analyze their practice.

To appropriately implement this growth-through-practice approach to professional development, the CASSST members must pay attention to two important issues. First, each member must be familiar with the techniques under study and be committed to learning the techniques. Second, each member must be knowledgeable about how to rehearse and be willing to participate in the learning process.

Types of Collegial Rehearsals

CASSST members rehearse in progressive rehearsals, each designed to engage teachers in thinking about various aspects of the delivery of instruction. As they move through the different types of rehearsals, teachers become more sophisticated in the ways they think about instruction. The kinds of rehearsals are *line rehearsal, block rehearsal*, and *dress rehearsal*. The effectiveness of all rehearsals depends on members' abilities and commitment to observing their teaching performances and reflecting upon their instructional efforts. Marilyn vos Savant says it simply: To acquire knowledge, one must study; but to acquire wisdom, one must observe.[4]

Line Rehearsal. In the first kind of rehearsal, the CASSST focuses on studying a technique or strategy to understand its subtleties and the conditions for appropriate use. The function of line rehearsals is analogous to learning lines in a play or isolating and practicing a routine or skill in sports until it becomes automatic. In other words, members of the CASSST create the script for the instruction and conduct the script with each other, refining words, directions, phrases, questions, movements, etc. Members do such study in order to create consistency in classroom delivery.

Like all rehearsals, line rehearsals should take place in safe settings where teachers can make and correct mistakes without being concerned about the effect of their instructional performance on students. Line rehearsals continue until the CASSST members become comfortable about their understanding of the technique, how to use it, why to use it, and when to use it appropriately.[5] The planning conference of the collegial coaching cycle can be used to focus the inquiry. Line rehearsals continue until the CASSST has confidence that all members possess the ability to execute consistently the technique or strategy. The CASSST then moves on to prepare lessons and study how specific techniques can be integrated into an instructional strategy, process, or method. This is done in the same way a gymnast would add a new technique to his or her tumbling routine. Teacher learning continues and moves to a more comprehensive rehearsal.

Illustration of the Line Rehearsal. CASSST members decide to develop their abilities to use questions more precisely with learners, specifically to focus on helping students think more deeply about their responses to questions. Members agree on a resource that will help them in their study, in this case *Learning to Question, Questioning to Learn*. In reading the book, the teachers agree that using follow-up questions, referred to as *processing questions* in the book, would benefit learners in processing information.

The group meets to discuss types of processing questions, their function, and appropriate phrasing and the kinds of responses they should elicit. When the members understand the nature and function of processing questions, together they devise ways of asking each other processing questions and practice using them with each other to get the "feel" of the questions, as well as to listen to the kinds of responses each type of question elicits.

One type of processing question, the *refocusing question*, requires that the questioner focus on three aspects in constructing the question. First, she or he must tell the respondent what was inappropriate about their answer. Second, the questioner must explain why the response was inappropriate. Finally, the questioner must restate the question. An example of a refocusing question is: You gave me an example of a horizontal line, the top of the table. I asked for a definition of horizontal, so what are some other words for horizontal? Phrasing each part of the refocusing question in a simple, straightforward, uncomplicated way takes time and reflection. The questioner needs to listen critically to the response to the redirected question to assure that it corresponds to the question criteria.

The Planning Conference Question Guide (see page 66) of the Collegial Coaching Cycle can assist the CASSST in their discussions about processing questions and guide them in planning a lesson appropriate for all the teachers to use during blocking rehearsal. It can direct teachers' reflection upon why each processing question is important to student learning and what problems they may encounter while demonstrating the processing questions. Additionally, the question guide can assist teachers in building theories about a technique or strategy that can be tested out with learners.

Each member of the CASSST in turn tries out the processing questions, while other members of the CASSST act as respondents. Each tryout should last one or two minutes. The CASSST also may choose to record tryouts for playback in order to more easily analyze each one. Recording tryouts allows members to participate both as questioners and respondents. Assuming both roles helps teachers study how the teacher thinks in order to ask the questions and how students think in order to answer them.

This facilitates insight into how the questions function to help students process information.

The CASSST collects information for analysis while viewing and/or listening to recordings of tryouts by observing and taking notes, focusing particularly on the use of processing questions. The teachers may count each time a certain processing question, such as a clarifying question, is asked appropriately, or how many times the teacher used a redirecting question to elicit answers from more than one participant. They may note the absence of the use of particular processing questions. They may determine that a teacher asked closed questions instead of open questions, jotting down the phrasing of the questions. Open questions should contain words like *what* or *how.*

Following the tryout or after observed recording, the CASSST provides feedback to the tryout teacher about his or her demonstration of processing questions. Using their notes, they indicate the successes the teacher had and the areas that need improvement. The goal of the line rehearsal is to learn the script and to invent classroom applications of a technique or strategy. In this case, the script is types of processing questions, how to phrase them appropriately so that respondents have an opportunity to think through their ideas, and what kind of response should be elicited for each particular processing question. The CASSST continues with line rehearsal until all the members have "learned their lines"how to ask each processing question and why each is important in guiding student thinking. Once that happens, the CASSST is ready to study processing questioning in a block rehearsal.

Block Rehearsal. For the second type of rehearsal, the CASSST focuses on the relationships between teachers' use of instructional techniques and their effect on the recipients of the instruction. In this setting, the CASSST identifies a series of discreet techniques to practice and analyze in simulated lessons. Again, this is a learning process for teachers. They should feel safe to make mistakes and to talk freely about the conditions necessary for delivering quality instruction.

During block rehearsals, CASSST members record their teaching episodes and engage in instructional conversations about these episodes. When preparing common lessons for conducting a teaching episode, the CASSST may use the planning conference of the collegial coaching cycle to structure their conversations (see the Planning Conference Question Guide on page 66). With each member of the CASSST alternating as teacher and learner, video or audio tapes of teaching episodes are recorded by the team. A teaching episode should last no more than 10 minutes. Observations and analysis focus on the series of techniques within the simulated lesson that were identified for practice earlier. The teacher in each teaching episode does a reflection on his or her teaching episode using the Reflection Time Question Guide on page 77. Once the reflection is completed, each CASSST member shares his or her teaching episodes and reflections with other team members for further analysis. Emphasis of the dialogue is on fine tuning techniques as they unfold within the delivery. The Debriefing Conference Question Guide on page 84 can be used to organize the inquiry.

Collegial dialogue during block rehearsals tends to scrutinize the relationship between implementation of a particular technique and the effect it has upon the recipients. At this point, members can generate hypotheses about teaching and learning that can be further tested in subsequent rehearsals. Block rehearsals should continue until members of the CASSST are confident that they can execute the strategy with their students. Again, it is important to note that the focus of practice and conversation in the block rehearsal is still on attaining control over instructional techniques. The block rehearsal, like the line rehearsal, is designed to assist classroom educators in investigating more deeply the relationships between preparing and conducting techniques. The effect techniques may have upon the recipients is considered. During block rehearsals, the CASSST incubates and articulates practice theories that may arise through the rehearsal, which in turn may influence their use of strategies with classroom learners.

Illustration of the Block Rehearsal. The CASSST meets to draft an exemplary lesson using processing questions, with particular attention paid to phrasing, predicting responses, managing space and timing, positioning in relation to persons answering questions, and sequencing processing questions to best solicit deeper thinking from participants. Once again, the Planning Conference Question Guide of the Collegial Coaching Cycle can assist the CASSST in structuring a lesson appropriate for all the teachers to use in tryouts. It also helps teachers reflect upon how they can use the processing questions more appropriately in their content areas and predict possible troublesome spots they may encounter while demonstrating the lesson with each other and with students.

Each member of the CASSST then takes a turn in trying out part of the lesson, with one teacher taking over where the previous teacher left off. Tryouts should last two minutes, since the data collected in a longer tryout would be overwhelming to analyze. These tryouts are simulations of classroom instruction that enable the members to focus on their instructional behavior without the encumbrance of having to teach while they learn the techniques. The CASSST should record the lesson tryouts for playback in order to analyze each person's tryout. This allows all members to participate in the tryout lesson and then collect data about all the tryouts.

The CASSST observes each teacher conducting a part of the lesson and takes notes, focusing particularly on the responses to questions, the order in which question are asked, and positioning in relation to respondents. Study of processing questions in the block rehearsal is more complex. Teachers must design a way to record more complicated actions. For example, for question sequence, they must devise a chart to collect and communicate the sequence of questions used during each teacher's tryout. To collect information about question/answer correspondence, the CASSST must find a way to designate the relationship between questions asked and responses given. One suggestion is to use a chart and codes for both teacher questions and participant responses, which is illustrated in the following table.

Teacher Question	cl	vr		rd		cl	rf	vr
Student Response	cl	vr	vr	vr	vr	vr	cl	vr

In this example, the *cl* stands for clarifying question or response, the *vr* indicates a verifying question or response, the *rd* stands for redirecting question, and the *rf* is a code for the refocusing question. From the coding in this chart, it can be determined that the teacher asking the processing questions is achieving question/answer correspondence to all questions except one. The teacher asks for clarification and the respondent gives a verification response and example instead of a definition. The teacher appropriately refocuses the response and clarification is elicited. The teacher also receives two verifying response, redirects the verifying question, and receives two more verifying responses without prompting the respondent with verifying questions.

Analysis during the block rehearsal can become very sophisticated, as the CASSST more intensely studies a technique or strategy. Using the Debriefing Conference Question Guide can help teachers distinguish the critical elements of a technique or strategy that must be honed before using it with learners. In this example, CASSST members are demonstrating to each other how processing questions function in a lesson, not just asking random questions. Teachers are responsible not only for asking a particular question with finesse, but also for deciding which question to ask next in order to extend the student's thinking based upon the responses they have already received. In rigorous study of the technique or strategy, teachers will refine areas that will help them be more adept in delivering instruction using the technique or strategy in the classroom. Likewise, they will test their assumptions and theories about teaching and learning, reflecting upon valuable information that will inform them about student learning and add to their instructional repertoires. The outcome of the block rehearsal is for CASSST members to develop further insights into the application of techniques and strategies, as well as temper the application of methods so that they become second nature. The block rehearsals continue until CASSST members feel comfortable enough to apply the method with learners. As teachers become more sophisticated in their understanding of the use of their methods, they will become more masterful in the connections they make between teaching and learning. They will begin to see how they are generators of theories that can be tested out in practice. In essence, they will be more informed about how practice influences theory and how theory can guide them in their instructional practices.

Dress Rehearsal. During the third kind of rehearsal the CASSST attempts to play out teacher learning and thinking within the context of their own classrooms. Again, while the delivery takes place with learners, it is an opportunity for teacher learning. During dress rehearsals, the CASSST may prepare their lessons together; however, each member carries out his or her lesson singularly in the classroom. Each teacher records the lesson, reflects upon the delivery, and isolates a small teaching episode. This episode may be one with which the teacher had difficulty and about which he or she would like to attain more insight, or it may be a section of the lesson that the teacher successfully executed and would like to share his or her insights with the rest of the team. This rehearsal brings to light issues not anticipated during prior rehearsals, since these did not include students. While the dress rehearsal is not intended as a forum for teaching content and skills to learners, students can profit from the experience of watching their teachers study their own instruction. As teachers continue to learn, so do learners.

Finally, the CASSST meets to study each other's selected teaching episodes in a debriefing conference. The outcome of the third rehearsal determines the need for the CASSST to further refine the techniques or strategy under study or to move on to investigate other techniques or instructional strategies. The debriefing conference questions are useful for gathering critical information the CASSST members will need to fine tune their techniques and further comprehend relationships they are forming between teaching and learning.

Illustration of the Dress Rehearsal. Everything the CASSST learned in their collaborative study comes together in the dress rehearsal, the testing ground for how the technique or strategy works with students. The focus of this rehearsal is for the teachers to collect information as to how well the strategies work to enhance student learning. It is also an opportunity for teachers to gather information about trouble spots in the techniques or strategies. In the example of lessons focused on using processing questions, each teacher in the CASSST plans a lesson appropriate for his or her students. They conduct the lesson and record it for later reflection and analysis. This is a learning experience for the teacher to study an instructional technique or strategy. While students may be engaged in learning something, the teacher's focus is on his or her execution of the method.

Once the lesson is completed, each teacher views his or her own lesson and writes a review of the lesson using the Reflection Time Question Guide (see page 77). The CASSST meets to view a particular episode of the recording to provide feedback to each teacher regarding problem areas or exemplary uses of the technique or strategy. In terms of processing questioning, a CASSST member may choose to show part of the lesson that created problems in the classroom for the students. For example, a common problem for teachers conducting a lesson with processing questions is how to provide opportunities for more than one student to respond to any question.

Using the Debriefing Conference Question Guide, other CASSST members lead a discussion, assisting the teacher who presented his or her recording in a problem-solving session. They ask questions to focus the teacher on the problem and to come up with solutions to his or her own troublesome area. In problem solving, teachers create opportunities for each other to see more deeply into how techniques or strategies operate to produce productive student learning. For example, by asking a teacher who wants to discover how to engage more student-to-student participation, debriefing questions like "Why do you think it is necessary to have more student-to-student interactions?" or "How could you arrange your students differently so that they will be more likely to talk to one another?" help teachers realize the relationships between their instructional behaviors and the effect their behaviors have on student participation. When teachers focus on the relationships between teaching and learning, their understanding of quality instruction increases. They are more likely to view the delivery of instruction analytically. Becoming more analytical and strategic about instructional delivery provides the threshold for educational excellence in our schools.

In closing, the more teachers work together to study and investigate their practices, the greater learning results they will have with their students. As teachers realize the value of professional learning, inside and outside of their classrooms, they become more skillful in their capacities to discern effective instruction. Together they build techniques and strategies that are contextually appropriate for their students, and they learn how to engage their colleagues in talent development. Not only are they teachers who teach well, they also are teacher educators who are masterful in effecting quality outcomes for their school community. This is teacher leadership.

Notes

1. John Dewey, *Democracy and Education: An Introduction to the Philosophy of Education* (New York: The Free Press, 1966).

2. Peter Senge, *Schools That Learn* (New York: Doubleday, 2000).

3. Marylou Dantonio and Paul Beisenherz, *Learning to Question, Questioning to Learn: Developing Effective Teacher Questioning Practices* (Needham Heights, Mass.: Allyn & Bacon, 2001).

4. Lorne A. Adrain, comp., *The Most Important Thing I Know* (New York: Cader Books, 1997), p. 16.

5. Ann Lieberman and Lynne Miller, *Teachers Transforming Their World and Their Work* (New York: Teachers College Press, 1999).

CHAPTER SIXTEEN

Summary

Collegial coaching is a collaborative, self-initiating, egalitarian approach to professional development, a process that facilitates opportunities for teachers to engage as professionals in inquiry and dialogue about instruction. It is based on a performing arts model of talent development. As teachers engage in inquiry and experimentation with instructional techniques and styles, they attain a sense of control over instructional problems that surface during classroom instruction. Collegial coaching offers teachers chances to try different teaching methods, to investigate techniques and strategies that are contextually conducive to student learning, and to give and receive objective comments in a nonevaluative setting. It is an empowering process that encourages and rewards inquiry into professional growth and emerging teacher leadership. Collegial coaching, as a form of continual, on-site faculty development, provides the impetus for teacher self-direction in professional development.

Collegial rehearsals extend the coaching process a means for groups of teachers to inquire into and study their teaching practices. Using collegial rehearsals, classroom educators can create more dynamic conceptions of quality instruction as they engage in learning about instructional delivery. Collegial Analysis Self-Study Support Teams (CASSST) can employ the collegial coaching process to create more conscious approaches to learning about teaching and inspire teachers to think about instruction in ways that sponsor effective, contextual instruction for their learners.

The collegial coaching process emphasizes the collaborative development of teachers' instructional talents rather than the evaluation of teachers. The process provides opportunities for teachers to talk about instructional goals and practices in order to develop shared visions about effective instruction. The cycle of collegial coaching has four phases:

- Planning Conference
- Observation of Teaching Performance
- Reflection Time
- Debriefing Conference

Each of the phases has a particular purpose. Teachers may choose to engage in one or all of the phases of the cycle.

The purpose of the planning conference is for the coaching partners or CASSST to prepare for instruction. They discuss the intended goals of a lesson or instructional technique, specify and sequence the instructional events, identify problems that may arise in instructional delivery, and determine strategies for dealing with anticipated problems. In collaboration, teachers select specific behaviors or techniques for the coach or CASSST to observe during classroom delivery or instructional practice, and they settle on an observation instrument to be used for this purpose.

During the observation of teaching performance, the coach or CASSST observes the behavior or technique that was specified in the planning conference and records it. Reflection time provides coaching partners or CASSST members a period of time to deliberate separately on the instructional actions so that they discover important relationships between teaching and learning. In the debriefing conference, the coaching partners or CASSST members share their insights and begin a problem-solving process to effect changes in the coached teacher's instructional practices. The focus of the debriefing conference is on the discrepancy between what teachers pictured or visualized would happen in preparing for instruction and what actually happened.

Throughout the collegial coaching cycle, teachers strive to concentrate on the development of a teaching repertoire for the delivery of effective instruction. It is a reflective process resulting in the use of problem solving as a method for informing teaching practice. By engaging in honest, open, nonjudgmental comments, the coaching partners or team members become knowing and confident about their instructional endeavors. Their attention to investigating instruction produces a productive learning environment for studying teaching. Likewise, their learning promotes quality instruction for their students.

Collegial coaching also contributes to building a school team focused on common instructional issues. As teachers develop a spirit of camaraderie, they are more likely to reach out to each other to solve classroom problems affecting student learning. They also may use the collegial coaching process to generate practice-based theories of instruction. By collaborating, teachers become active agents in shaping the instructional talents of their colleagues.

Teacher instructional leadership is emergent. Empowering teacher leadership is directly related to administrators' attitudes about teacher development and establishing collegial school climates conducive to inquiry and experimentation with instructional practice. The school principal is instrumental in instituting a pedagogically sound collegial coaching program and must be supportive of teachers' analyses of their instruction. The principal must be knowledgeable about the collegial coaching process, supportive of teachers in their study of teaching, and flexible in arranging time and space for teachers to observe each other and confer about instructional practices. This means that principals must change their leadership role from one of power and authority over teachers to shared leadership with teachers. By cultivating a school climate of shared leadership, principals can establish the necessary conditions for building camaraderie among school educators in their pursuit of effective instruction for students. These conditions are based on the following premises:

- No one can force another person to change his or her teaching behavior.
- Instructional improvement relies on objective, descriptive reporting of teaching behaviors.
- Reflective practices and problem solving are on-going processes of professional growth.
- Collaboration among educators in a school community is a process of attraction.
- Time for teacher collaboration is important enough to be included in the school schedule.

A successful collegial coaching program, implemented either by coaching partners or teams, reduces the stress of teaching by facilitating a safe environment for practicing and sharing teaching practices. Teachers can enhance and refine a repertoire of instructional practices by and through the support of other teachers. Additionally, collegial coaching engages teachers in continual deliberation about the relationship between instructional practices and the effects of instruction on students' learning. This contributes to the formation of theories about instruction based in teaching practice. As teachers share their learning with each other, school morale improves and feelings of isolation diminish. Through collegial coaching, teachers empower each other to grow and lead in ways most appealing to them while they improve and enhance classroom instruction for children—the center of their professional lives.

REFERENCES

Adrain, Lorne A., comp. *The Most Important Thing I Know*. New York: Cader Books, 1997.

Anastos, Joy, and Robert Ancowitz. "A Teacher-Directed Peer Coaching Project." *Educational Leadership* 44, no. 3 (1987): 40-42.

Anderson, Robert H., and Karolyn J. Snyder, eds. *Clinical Supervision: Coaching for Higher Performance*. Lancaster, Penn.: Technomic Publishing Company, Inc., 1993.

Ashton, Patricia T. "Teacher Efficacy: A Motivational Paradigm for Effective Teacher Education." *Journal of Teacher Education* 35, no. 5 (1984): 28-32.

Ashton, Patricia T., and Rodman B. Webb. *Making a Difference: Teachers' Sense of Efficacy and Student Achievement*. New York: Longman, 1986.

Ashton, Patricia T., Rodman B. Webb, and Nancy Doda. *A Study of Teachers' Sense of Efficacy: Final Report, Executive Summary*. Gainesville, Fla.: Foundations of Education, University of Florida, 1983.

Ball, Deborah Loewenberg, and David K. Cohen. "Developing Practice, Developing Practitioners: Toward a Practice-Based Theory of Professional Education." In *Teaching As the Learning Profession: Handbook of Policy and Practice*. Edited by Linda Darling-Hammond and Gary Sykes. San Francisco: Jossey-Bass, 1999.

Bandura, Albert. "Self-Efficacy: Toward a Unifying Theory of Behavioral Change." *Psychological Review* 84, no. 2 (1977): 191-215.

Berliner, David C. "The Development of Expertise in Pedagogy." Charles W. Hunt Memorial Lecture presented at the annual meeting of the American Association for Colleges of Teacher Education, New Orleans, February 1988.

Beyer, Barry K. *Practical Strategies for the Teaching of Thinking*. Boston: Allyn & Bacon, 1987.

Bissex, Glenda L., and Richard H. Bullock. Seeing for Ourselves: Case Study Research by Teachers of Writing. Portsmouth, N.H.: Heinemann, 1987.

Bohm, David. *On Dialogue*. Edited by Lee Nichol. London: Routledge, 1996.

Borko, Hilda, and Carol Livingston. "Cognition and Improvisation: Differences in Mathematics Instruction by Expert and Novice Teachers." *American Educational Research Journal* 26, no. 4 (1989): 473-98.

Broom, Elizabeth. "A Study of Peer Coaching and the Relationship between Teacher Efficacy and Stages of Concern." Ph.D. diss., University of New Orleans, 1994.

Calderhead, James. "The Quality of Reflection in Student Teachers' Professional Learning." *European Journal of Teacher Education* 10, no. 3 (1987): 269-78.

Calderhead, James, and Peter Gates. "Introduction." In Conceptualizing Reflection in *Teacher Development*. Edited by J. James Calderhead and Peter Gates. London: Falmer Press, 1993.

Carr, Wilfred, and Stephen Kemmis. *Becoming Critical: Education, Knowledge and Action Research*. London: Falmer Press, 1986.

Carter, Kathy, et al. "Processing and Using Information about Students: A Study of Expert, Novice and Postulant Teachers." *Teaching and Teacher Education* 3, no. 2 (1987): 147-57.

Chatterjee, Debashis. *Leading Consciously: A Pilgrimage Toward Self-Mastery*. Boston: Butterworth-Heinemann, 1998.

Childre, Doc Lew, and Bruce Cryer. *From Chaos to Coherence: Advancing Emotional and Organizational Intelligence Through Inner Quality Management*. Boston: Butterworth-Heinemann, 1999.

Clark, Christopher M., and Penelope L. Peterson. "Teachers' Thought Processes." In *Handbook of Research on Teaching*. 3rd ed. Edited by Merlin C. Wittrock. New York: Macmillan, 1986, pp. 255-96.

Clark, Christopher, and Robert Yinger. "Teacher Planning." *In Exploring Teacher Thinking.* Edited by James Calderhead. London: Cassell, 1987, pp. 84-103.

Cochran-Smith, Marilyn, and Susan L. Lytle. "Research on Teaching and Teacher Research: The Issues That Divide." *Educational Researcher* 19, no. 2 (1990): 2-11.

———. *Inside/Outside: Teacher Research and Knowledge.* New York: Teachers College Press, 1993.

Cole, Ardra L., and J. Gary Knowles. *Researching Teaching: Exploring Teacher Development Through Reflexive Inquiry.* Boston: Allyn & Bacon, 2000.

Connelly, F. Michael, and D. Jean Clandinin. *Teachers As Curriculum Planners: Narratives of Experience.* New York: Teachers College Press, 1988.

Cooper, Bruce S., John E. Iorio, and John Poster. "Organizing Schools for Teacher Collegiality: The New York City Experience." *Education* 111, no. 1 (1990): 68-76.

Costa, Arthur L. "How World-Class Standards Will Change Us." *Educational Leadership* 50, no. 5 (1993): 50-51.

Costa, Arthur L., and Robert Garmston. *Another Set of Eyes: Conference Skills Part II.* Educational consultants Arthur Costa and Robert Garmston. 40 min. Association for Supervision and Curriculum Development, 1989. Videocassette.

———. "The Art of Cognitive Coaching: Supervision for Intelligent Teaching." Training syllabus. Institute for Intelligent Behavior, Sacramento, Cal., 1990.

———. "Coaching Elegance." Paper presented at the annual meeting of the Association for Supervision and Curriculum Development, New Orleans, April 1992.

———. *Cognitive Coaching: A Foundation for Renaissance Schools.* Norwood, Mass.: Christopher Gordon Publishers, 1994.

Danielson, Charlotte. *Teacher Evaluation to Enhance Professional Development.* Alexandria, Va.: Association for Supervision and Curriculum Development, 2000.

Dantonio, Marylou. *Teachers Coaching Teachers: Instructional Leadership through Empowering Teachers.* Bloomington, Ind.: Phi Delta Kappa, 1988.

———. *How Can We Create Thinkers? Questioning Strategies that Work for Teachers.* Bloomington, Ind.: National Educational Service, 1990.

———. *Teacher Professionalism and Leadership in Louisiana: A Resource Manual.* Baton Rouge, La.: Louisiana Department of Education, 1992.

———. "Portraits in Teaching: Documenting Teacher Development through Portfolios." *Louisiana Social Studies Journal* 19, no. 1 (1992): 20-24.

Dantonio, Marylou, and Paul Beisenherz. *Learning to Question: Questioning to Learn.* Needham, Mass.: Allyn & Bacon, 2001.

Dantonio, Marylou, and James Randels. "Differences in Pedagogical Thought Processes Used in Planning, Conducting, and Reflecting by Novice and Experienced English Teachers." Paper presented at the annual conference of the Association of Teacher Educators, New Orleans, February 1991).

Darling-Hammond, Linda, and Gary Sykes, eds. *Teaching As the Learning Profession: Handbook of Policy and Practice.* San Francisco: Jossey-Bass, 1999.

Deal, Terrence, and Kent D. Peterson. *Shaping School Culture: The Heart of Leadership.* San Francisco: Jossey-Bass, 1999.

Dembo, Myron H., and Sherri Gibson. "Teachers' Sense of Efficacy: An Important Factor in School Improvement." *Elementary School Journal* 86, no. 2 (1985): 173-84.

Desrochers, Cynthia G., and Sheryll R. Klein. "Teacher-Directed Peer Coaching As a Follow-Up to Staff Development." *Journal of Staff Development* 11, no. 2 (1990): 6-10.

Dewey, John. *The Relation of Theory to Practice in Education. The Third Yearbook of the National Society for the Study of Education, Part I.* Chicago, Ill.: University of Chicago Press, 1904.

———. *Experience and Education.* New York: Macmillan, 1938.

————. *Democracy and Education: An Introduction to the Philosophy of Education.* New York: The Free Press, 1966.

DuFour, Richard, and Robert Eaker. *Professional Learning Communities at Work.* Bloomington, Ind.: National Education Service, 1998.

Eisner, Eliot W. "Why Standards May Not Improve Schools." *Educational Leadership* 50, no. 5 (1993): 22-23.

Elbaz, Freema. "The Teachers' 'Practical Knowledge': Report of a Case Study." *Curriculum Inquiry* 11, no. 1 (1981): 43-71.

Freire, Paulo. *The Politics of Education: Culture, Power, and Liberation.* South Hadley, Mass.: Bergin and Garvey, 1985.

Garman, Noreen B. "Reflection, the Heart of Clinical Supervision: A Modern Rationale for Professional Practice." *Journal of Curriculum and Supervision* 2, no.1 (1986): 1-24.

Garmston, Robert. "How Administrators Support Peer Coaching." *Educational Leadership* 44, no. 2 (1987): 19-26.

Gibson, Sherri, and Myron H. Dembo. "Teacher Efficacy: A Construct Validation." *Journal of Educational Psychology* 76, no. 4 (1984): 569-82.

Gitlin, Andrew. "Understanding Teaching Dialogically." *Teachers College Record* 91, no. 4 (1990): 537-63.

Gitlin, Andrew, and Karen Price. "Teacher Empowerment and the Development of Voice." In *Supervision in Transition.* Edited by Carl D. Glickman. Alexandria, Va.: Association for Supervision and Curriculum Development, 1992.

Good, Thomas L., and Jere E. Brophy. *Looking in Classrooms.* 4th ed. New York: Harper and Row, 1987.

Goswami, D. Dixie, and Peter Stillman. *Reclaiming the Classroom: Teacher Research As an Agency for Change.* Upper Montclair, N.J.: Boynton/Cook, 1987.

Grimmett, Peter P., Olaf P. Rostad, and Blake Ford. "The Transformation of Supervision." In *Supervision in Transition.* Edited by Carl D. Glickman. Alexandria, Va.: Association for Supervision and Curriculum Development, 1992.

Guskey, Thomas R. "Context Variables That Affect Measures of Teacher Efficacy." *Journal of Educational Research* 81, no. 1 (1987): 41-47.

Hargreaves, Andy, and Ruth Dawe. "Paths of Professional Development: Contrived Collegiality, Collaborative Culture, and the Case of Peer Coaching." *Teaching and Teacher Education* 6, no. 3 (1990): 227-41.

Hargreaves, Andy, and Michael G. Fullan. *Understanding Teacher Development.* New York: Teachers College Press, 1992.

Martin Huberman. "Networks That Alter Teaching: Conceptualizations, Exchanges, and Experiments." *Teachers and Teaching: Theory and Practice* 1, no. 2 (1995): 193-211.

James, Susan, Daniel Heller, and William Ellis. "Peer Assistance in a Small District: Windham Southeast, Vermont." In *Supervision in Transition.* Edited by Carl D. Glickman. Alexandria, Va.: Association for Supervision and Curriculum Development, 1992.

Joyce, Bruce, and Beverly Showers. "Improving Inservice Training: The Messages of Research." *Educational Leadership* 37, no. 5 (1980): 379-85.

————. "The Coaching of Teaching." *Educational Leadership* 40, no. 1 (1982): 4-8, 10.

————. *Student Achievement through Staff Development.* New York: Longman, 1988.

Katzman, Martin T. *The Political Economy of Urban Schools.* Cambridge, Mass.: Harvard University Press, 1971.

Kennedy, Mary M. "Establishing Professional Schools for Teachers." In *Professional Practice Schools:*

Linking Teacher Education and School Reform. Edited by Marsha Levine. New York: Teachers College Press, 1992.

Krug, Samuel E. "Leadership Craft and the Crafting of School Leaders." *Phi Delta Kappan* 75, no. 3 (1993): 240-44.

Lampert, Magdalene. "How Do Teachers Manage to Teach? Perspectives on Problems in Practice." *Harvard Educational Review* 55, no. 2, (1985): 178-94.

Leinhardt, Gaea. *Novice and Expert Knowledge of Individual Student's Achievement.* A report of research conducted by the Pennsylvania Learning Research and Development Center, University of Pittsburgh, for the National Institute of Education, Washington, D.C., 1983, ERIC No. ED 233 985.

———. "Math Lessons: A Contrast of Novice and Expert Competence." Journal for Research in Mathematics Education 20, no. 1 (1989): 52-75.

Leinhardt, Gaea, and Ralph T. Putnam. "Profile of Expertise in Elementary School Mathematics Teaching." *Arithmetic Teacher* 34, no. 2 (1986): 8-29.

Levine, Marsha. "A Conceptual Framework for Professional Practice Schools." In *Professional Practice Schools: Linking Teacher Education and School Reform.* Edited by Marsha Levine. New York: Teachers College Press, 1992.

Lieberman, Ann. "Expanding the Leadership Team." *Educational Leadership* 45, no. 5 (1988): 4-8.

Lieberman, Ann, and Lynne Miller. *Teachers, Their World, and Their Work: Implications for School Improvement.* Alexandria, Va.: Association for Supervision and Curriculum Development, 1984.

———. "Teacher Development in Professional Practice Schools." In *Professional Practice Schools: Linking Teacher Education and School Reform.* Edited by Marsha Levine. New York: Teachers College Press, 1992.

———. *Teachers Transforming Their World and Their Work.* New York: Teachers College Press, 1999.

———, eds. *Staff Development: New Demands, New Realities, New Perspectives.* New York: Teachers College Press, 1979.

Little, Judith W. "Norms of Collegiality and Experimentation: Workplace Conditions of School Success." *American Educational Research Journal* 19, no. 3 (1982): 325-40.

———. "Seductive Images and Organizational Realities in Professional Development." In *Rethinking School Improvement: Research, Craft, and Concept.* Edited by Ann Lieberman. New York: Teachers College Press, 1986.

Livingston, Carol, and Hilda Borko. "Expert-Novice Differences in Teaching: A Cognitive Analysis and Implications for Teacher Education." *Journal of Teacher Education* 40, no. 4 (1989): 36-42.

Lugg, Catherine A., and William L. Boyd. "Leadership for Collaboration: Reducing Risk and Fostering Resilience." *Phi Delta Kappan* 75, no. 3 (1993): 253-58.

Maehr, Martin L., and Stephanie A. Parker. "A Tale of Two Schools—and the Primary Task of Leadership." *Phi Delta Kappan* 75, no. 3 (1993): 233-39.

McNiff, Jean. *Teaching As Learning: An Action Research Approach.* London: Routledge Press, 1993.

———. *You and Your Action Research.* London: Routledge Press, 1996.

Mohr, Marion M., and Marions Maclean. *Working Together: A Guide for Teacher-Researchers.* Urbana, Ill.: National Council of Teachers of English, 1987.

Moffett, Kenneth, Jane St. John, and Joann Isken. "Training and Coaching Beginning Teachers: An Antidote to Reality Shock." *Educational Leadership* 44, no. 2 (1987): 34-36.

Munro, Petra, and Jack Elliott. "Instructional Growth through Peer Coaching." *Journal of Staff Development* 8, no. 1 (1987): 25-28.

Nolan, James, and Pam Francis. "Changing Perspectives in Curriculum and Instruction." In *Supervision in Transition.* Edited by Carl D. Glickman. Alexandria, Va.: Association for Supervision and

Curriculum Development, 1992.

Nolan, Jim, Brent Hawkes, and Pam Francis. "Case Studies: Windows onto Clinical Supervision." *Educational Leadership* 51, no. 2 (1993): 52-56.

Oliva, Peter F. *Supervision for Today's Schools.* 3rd ed. New York: Longman, 1989.

O'Neil, John. "Supervision Reappraised." *ASCD UPDATE* 35, no. 6 (1993): 1, 3, 8.

Osterman, Karen F. "Reflective Practice: A New Agenda for Education." *Education and Urban Society* 22, no. 2 (1990): 133-52.

Osterman, Karen F., and R. Robert B. Kottkamp. *Reflective Practice for Educators: Improving Schooling Through Professional Development.* Newbury Park, Calif.: Corwin Press, 1993.

Peterson, Penelope L., and Michelle A. Comeaux. "Teachers' Schemata for Classroom Events: The Mental Scaffolding of Teachers' Thinking during Classroom Instruction." *Teaching and Teacher Education* 3, no. 4 (1987): 319-31.

Poole, Wendy L. "Removing the Super from Supervision." *Journal of Curriculum and Supervision* 9, no. 3 (1994): 284-309.

Robbins, Pamela. *How to Plan and Implement a Peer Coaching Program.* Alexandria, Va.: Association for Supervision and Curriculum Development, 1991.

Rosenholtz, Susan J. *Teachers' Workplace: The Social Organization of Schools.* New York: Longman, 1989.

Ross, John A. "Teacher Efficacy and the Effects of Coaching on Student Achievement." *Canadian Journal of Education* 17, no. 1(1992): 51-65.

Ross, Rick, Bryan Smith, and Charlotte Roberts. "The Team Learning Wheel." In *The Fifth Discipline Fieldbook: Strategies and Tools for Building a Learning Organization.* Edited by Peter Senge et al. New York : Doubleday, 1994.

Rubin, Louis. "The Thinking Teacher: Cultivating Pedagogical Intelligence." *Journal of Teacher Education* 40, no. 6 (1989): 31-34.

Sagor, Richard. *How to Conduct Collaborative Action Research.* Alexandria, Va.: Association for Supervision and Curriculum Development, 1992.

Sarason, Seymour B. *Teaching As a Performing Art.* New York: Teachers College Press, 1999.

Schon, Donald A. *The Reflective Practitioner: How Professionals Think in Action.* New York: Basic Books, 1983.

———. *Educating the Reflective Practitioner: Toward a New Design for Teaching and Learning in the Professions.* San Francisco: Jossey-Bass, 1987.

———. "Coaching Reflective Teaching." In *Reflection in Teacher Education.* Edited by Peter P. Grimmett and Gaalen L. Erickson. New York: Teachers College Press, 1988.

Senge, Peter. *The Fifth Discipline: The Art and Practice of the Learning Organization.* New York: Doubleday, 1990.

———. *Schools That Learn.* New York: Doubleday, 2000.

Sergiovanni, Thomas. "The Theoretical Basis for Cultural Leadership." In *Leadership: Examining the Elusive.* Edited by Linda Sheive and Marian B. Schoenheit. Alexandria, Va.: Association for Supervision and Curriculum Development, 1987.

Showers, Beverly. "Teachers Coaching Teachers." *Educational Leadership* 42, no. 7 (1985): 43-48.

Smith, Wilma F. "Leadership for Educational Renewal." *Phi Delta Kappan* 80, no. 8 (1999): 602-05.

Smith, Wilma F., and Richard L. Andrews. *Instructional Leadership: How Principals Make a Difference.* Alexandria, Va.: Association for Supervision and Curriculum Development, 1989.

Snyder, Karolyn J. "Schooling Transformation: The Context for Professional Coaching and Problem Solving." In *Clinical Supervision: Coaching for Higher Performance.* Edited by Robert H. Anderson and Karolyn J. Snyder. Lancaster, Pa.: Technomic Publishing Company, 1993.

Stevenson, Harold W. "Why Asian Students Still Outdistance Americans." *Educational Leadership* 50, no. 5, (1993): 63-65.

Thompson, Charles L., and John S. Zeuli. "The Frame and the Tapestry: Standards-Based Reform and Professional Development." In *Teaching As the Learning Profession: Handbook of Policy and Practice.* Edited by Linda Darling-Hammond and Gary Sykes. San Francisco: Jossey-Bass, 1999.

Turner, Barbara. "Accelerated Schools Successes." Speech delivered at the Louisiana Accelerated Schools Network, New Orleans, January 1994.

VanAssen, Linda A., and Saundra J. Tracy. "Using What We Know about Collegial Assistance." *Journal of Staff Development* 12, no. 4 (1991): 48-50.

Van Manen, Max. "Linking Ways of Knowing with Ways of Being Practical." *Curriculum Inquiry* 6, no. 3 (1977): 205-28.

Vygotsky, Lev S. *Mind in Society: The Development of Higher Psychological Process.* Edited by Michael Cole et al. Cambridge, Mass.: Harvard University Press, 1978.

Westerman, Delores A. "Expert and Novice Teacher Decision Making." *Journal of Teacher Education* 42, no. 4 (1991): 292-305.

Whitehead, Jack. "Creating a Living Educational Theory from Questions of the Kind, 'How Do I Improve My Practice?'" *Cambridge Journal of Education* 19, no.1 (1989): 41-52.

Wildman, Terry M., and Jerome A. Niles. "Reflective Teachers: Tensions between Abstractions and Realities." *Journal of Teacher Education* 38, no. 4 (1987): 25-31.

Yinger, Robert J. "A Study of Teacher Planning." *Elementary School Journal* 80, no. 3 (1980): 107-27.

———. "Learning the Language of Practice." Curriculum Inquiry 17, no. 3 (1987): 293-318.